P9-DZX-799

The Natural Wedding

The Natural *Wedding*

Ideas and Inspirations for a
Stylish and Green Celebration

Louise Moon

Universe

Contents

Foreword by Jo Wood

You want your wedding day to be the best day of your life, so why not plan it with an organic, eco-, and ethical conscience, ensuring your values and personality shine through. From sourcing a unique, one-off vintage dress to designing a locally sourced and seasonal menu, finding beautiful vintage crockery, or using a biodegradable tent, there really is an ecochoice out there for everyone.

The eco-option can also be kinder on the purse strings and offer you ways to make your day even more memorable, as I found when my daughter Leah got married in 2008. We used flowers from the garden and collected jam jars to use as water glasses instead of renting them. We even got a certificate from the council for all our recycling efforts.

If you don't have the time to research local vendors and grow your own, then why not approach a sustainable catering company to help get you started? I set up Mrs. Paisley's Lashings, with leading ecochef Arthur Potts Dawson, with this in mind. A percentage of our profits go toward funding gardens in schools, so we can encourage the next generation toward healthy, organic eating.

I'm delighted that Louise Moon is sharing her expertise in green weddings; we all need to be taking small steps toward a united, global environmental change, and where better to begin than your wedding. Why not start married life as you mean to go on?

I wish you all the very best with planning your big day; love your planet, go organic.

Jo Wood

Jo Wood, founder of Jo Wood Organics
London, 2010

Introduction

My love of all things green and gorgeous started at an organic bed-and-breakfast in Dorset, many years ago. My fiancé and I ate delicious organic breakfasts, enjoyed 100 percent–natural toiletries, browsed in the town's ethical shops, buying ecowares and natural shampoos and soaps, and left with changed priorities.

Not long after, I launched EcoMoon, my wedding-planning business with a difference, designed to offer people a stylish alternative to the carbon-heavy and usually very expensive standard wedding. Current figures show that the average wedding can send 14.5 tons of carbon dioxide into the atmosphere—roughly double an individual human's carbon footprint for a year! This results in an expensive day, both for a couple's pockets and for Earth. So what is the alternative? Well, that is where my book comes in.

I wanted to write *The Natural Wedding* to provide couples with inspiration and advice on every aspect of their greener celebration, from vintage gowns to seasonal flowers, from natural decorations to organic skin care, with gorgeous photographs to show their family and friends. As I have written it, I have included many hints and tips from my years of planning as well as projects to make at home—everything from organic cupcakes to wedding-day bags. It is my ecochic guide to weddings for all couples, regardless of budget. No hairy shirts or mud in sight!

The Natural Wedding is here to dispel the myth that an eco-conscious wedding can't be stylish and look exactly like a "regular" wedding, if that is what you wish for. Similarly, for couples wanting a unique, handmade day, then this is the book to show you how. With just a little effort and forethought, your celebration can be a fabulous and individual event that is a pleasure for you to plan.

So, now you have a copy of this book, I hope that you will enjoy using it and carry it with you to dip into whenever you need a little advice or inspiration. At the end, you will find a comprehensive directory of fabulous ecofriendly suppliers, artisan producers, and generally good people.

Remember, whether dreaming of a formal celebration in a fairy-tale castle or a festival-inspired event with tepees in the woods, planning a natural wedding should be enjoyable, stress free, and about starting your married lives with dainty footprints on Earth.

Have a happy wedding!

Louise Moon
Bath, July 2010

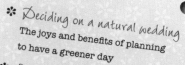

❋ *Deciding on a natural wedding*
The joys and benefits of planning to have a greener day

❋ *Seasonal weddings*
Choose your wedding style—from food to flowers—making the most of the time of year

❋ *Vintage weddings*
Go overboard with retro designs

❋ *Ecochic weddings*
Modern, minimalist, and couture

❋ *Handmade weddings*
Make your own wedding, with love and a wealth of creativity

❋ *Getting practical*
Budgeting and choosing your ceremony

❋ *Farther afield and precelebrations*
Plus greener ways to marry abroad

The Style

You've just gotten engaged—congratulations! And now you're thinking about the kind of wedding you would like. Maybe you've considered being greener, or perhaps you're searching for ideas to help your budget go further or to make your day truly special and unique. This chapter brings together themes and inspirations to engage your imagination, along with practical advice to help you on your way.

Deciding on a natural wedding

The beauty of deciding to have a naturally inspired wedding is the abundance of wonderful possibilities. For me, a natural wedding conjures up images of stunning, locally grown flowers and plants; flavorsome organic menus and artisan treats; gorgeous vintage bridal gowns and jewelry borrowed from friends or relatives; creative, handmade invitations; and relaxing, plant-based facials. And that is just the start.

Given half the chance, most couples would choose a green, natural, and ethical day, but in my experience, many simply do not know where to begin. You may already shop at your local farmers' market and take energy-saving measures at home, use natural cleaning and beauty products and buy fair trade whenever you can; but with so many choices to make when planning a wedding, along with the time pressures and the stress, it can often feel easier to go with the standard options.

The idea of this book is to give you some natural inspiration and to guide you through the information you'll need to make the choices that are best for you—and that are gentler on the environment.

Do just one thing . . .

I always say to couples planning their wedding, "If you can do just one thing. . ." and by this I mean one natural, ecofriendly, or ethical thing. It could be choosing seasonal food, lighting the tables with plant-wax candles, or honeymooning at an ecoboutique hotel. If every couple did this, it would make a real difference to the environmental impact of the wedding industry.

On average, a wedding puts 14.5 tons of carbon dioxide into the atmosphere—or twice your personal yearly carbon footprint. Food flown thousands of miles and travel by guests are the biggest factors. For peace of mind, consider the ethics and chemical content of some wedding products, too (see the Glossary on page 215).

> ### Greener venues
> Beaches, arboretums, village halls, charity-owned historic homes, parks, gardens, tepees, and yurts.

Natural inspiration

Being ecoaware doesn't mean a wedding in a scratchy dress and a muddy field (although a field can be an amazing location). You could have a supersoft, hemp-silk couture gown made for your ceremony, then hold a barbecue on a sweeping crescent of beach. Or, imagine brightly colored, people-powered rickshaws, a woodland clearing as your setting, and favor boxes made from wildflower-seed paper.

Choosing your wedding style

Spend time dipping into and choosing elements for your wedding style from the pages that follow. Whichever style you are drawn to, opt for organic and biodynamic food, grown according to ecofriendly guidelines, and fair-trade products that have been ethically made with the welfare of their producers in mind (see the Directory on page 208).

Knowing that your wedding is having a positive effect on the environment is the perfect way for you to start your married lives. So be different, personalize your day, and choose an unusual venue, homemade food, and a stunning ethical dress. You, your family, and your guests will have an unforgettable day.

> Wedding planner tip:
> As you plan, take pleasure from meeting like-minded people and discover your creative side—and, most important, have fun.

Seasonal weddings

From springtime tulips to brink-of-autumn echinaceas, make the most of seasonal flowers and foliage, and enjoy foods at the peak of their flavor. Fruit, vegetables, and flowers that can be grown naturally outdoors in your region reduce the need for preservatives or artificial climates. Local produce has less distance to travel and helps to reduce your wedding's carbon footprint.

Let the time of the year when you are marrying inspire your choice of wedding location and dress. Tents, tepees, and yurts are perfect for the summer, while ecochic hotels, historic homes, and modern green wedding venues suit cooler winter weather. Often, the surrounding landscape will present the best backdrops to your photographs. Link hands beneath blossoming trees for a natural confetti shot.

Food through the year

Hot comfort food, with rich sauces and deep flavors, will warm up winter-themed weddings. Light, fresh tastes, from tingling fruit sorbets to many-colored salads, are ideal for celebrations in the summer. Organically grown fruit and flowers avoid the synthetic pesticides that are common elsewhere in agriculture. If you find organic produce too expensive to buy, try growing your own (see page 112). Or discover food for free, by foraging for the likes of star-flowered wild garlic on a long country walk.

Making the seasons your wedding style

Any couple can have a celebration that is sensitive to the season, whether you already lead an ecofriendly lifestyle or not. Personalize your day with seasonal elements chosen for the time of year: natural fabrics, such as cool linen or gentle, wool knits; skin-care treats made with local strawberries (see page 180); or a bouquet of cornflowers you have tied yourself (see page 146). For timely themes, think of a country garden, autumn colors, the summer sun, a winter chill, spring blossoms, or a village fête.

All about flowers

Try making flowers—or even a single flower variety—the focus of your wedding design. It's a simple way to create an effortlessly coordinated look.

* Commission an artist to draw your chosen flower, and use the illustration for invitations, menus, and orders of service.
* Use the same kinds of flowers for your table decorations and bouquets.
* Break apart flower heads to make fresh petal confetti (see page 152).
* Ice a floral design onto homemade biscuits for your favors.
* Decorate your cake with fresh flower buds.
* Wear a single bloom in your hair.

Rich pickings

* Fresh-picked strawberries, blueberries, and raspberries
* Brightly colored squashes
* Winter root vegetables
* Homemade elderflower cordial
* Cider made from juicy, local apples
* Locally caught fish or free-range local meat in its prime season
* Homemade seasonal jams
* Home-baked cakes decorated with seasonal fruit or flowers
* Wildflowers grown in your garden
* Berries and seed heads for your decorations

Natural advantages

Locally grown, seasonal food and flowers mean fewer food miles and support local farmers and enterprises.

Vintage weddings

Indulge your vintage side and bring together all those little gems you've collected over the years: the beaded Italian bag; the fabulous 1950s wedding gown; the Edwardian pearl necklace; and the long, elegant gloves. Antique, secondhand, and reused items are great for the environment. They are effectively carbon neutral as they have already been used, and you may well be saving them from being thrown away.

Secondhand stores are a fantastic source of unexpected finds—buying from them will benefit both the good cause and your wallet. Relatives may also have heirloom jewelry, ceramics, or linen to pass down to you. Don't be afraid to use items that do not match—it can create a delightfully eclectic look.

Stylish couples
Take inspiration from these classic, twentieth-century weddings:
* Grace Kelly and Prince Rainier
    A fairy-tale wedding in Monaco in 1956, in front of the world's press and the adoring public. She wore a full-skirted gown, crafted from ivory silk taffeta and lace.
* Edward and Mrs. Simpson
    They married in 1937 in France, shortly after he renounced the British throne. She wore an elegant, cream-colored, long-sleeved skirt-suit, complete with neat, covered-button detailing, and a stylish hat, and carried a small matching bag.
* Yoko Ono and John Lennon
    Sixties fashion at its best. They married in Gibraltar in 1969; Yoko wore a white crêpe minidress, white kneesocks, and a wide-brimmed hat.

Setting up your own garden party
Marry in a local church, then walk to your reception in a friend's flower-filled garden. Decorate a traditional tent with homemade bunting and vintage vases filled with cottage-garden flowers. An elegant string quartet, or friends busking, is the perfect accompaniment. As the sun goes down, light soy candles in recycled jam jars.
* Hired furniture should be delivered the night before and stored under cover.
* Make sure there is enough room for people to walk between rows of chairs.
* Layering vintage tablecloths or spreading lengths of vintage sari fabric over plain white cloths will disguise ordinary tables.
* Arrange flowers the night before, then keep them somewhere cool and dark.

Style from the past
* Eclectic floral china
* Retro, 1960s colored-glass vases
* Antique suitcases
* Beautiful lace dresses
* Original printing stamps
* Chic vanity cases
* Vintage *Vogue* magazines
* Heavy linen tablecloths
* Heirloom veils
* Long white gloves
* Inherited jewelry
* Salvaged dress patterns

Natural advantages
Retro gowns, country-style tea parties, and florals—reusing is effectively carbon neutral and reduces what might otherwise go to waste.

Modern for less

❊ Beachcombed pebbles
   as place-card holders

❊ Single flower stems in
   recycled bottles

❊ Paperless designer e-vites
   (www.paperlesspost.com)

❊ Natural soaps for favors

❊ A simple, chic color
   scheme, such as stylish
   black and white

❊ White linen tablecloths

❊ A simple dress with
   contemporary ecojewelry

❊ Barbecue on the beach

❊ White-iced cupcakes
   on a rented, tiered stand

❊ Sky lanterns

❊ Cool camping for
   your honeymoon

Natural advantages

Green designer services often
focus on energy-saving ideas
and reusing and recycling, and
have strong ethical policies.

Ecochic weddings

From urban ecoboutique hotels to innovative organic catering, you can have a big day that is contemporary, chic, and green, too. There's no need to compromise your taste. Revel in the growing range of ecodesigner labels and bespoke makers, such as Jessica Charleston, who created the kimono-inspired dress on the opposite page (see the Directory on page 209). If you have a smaller budget, there are ways to create a sleek, modern look for less—take a look at the list on the left.

Ecostores and vendors can provide you with wedding products designed specifically to minimize your carbon impact. Most of these also have outstanding ethics. You can find everything from designer organic cakes to beautiful recycled paper stationery and artisan-made wooden place cards.

Simplicity itself

Fill straight-sided, contemporary glass bowls with organic white roses for minimalist floral displays; choose modern, ethical fabrics such as hemp silk (see page 64); decorate tables with driftwood; and have a clean-lined, white-iced artisan-made cake, decorated with artfully placed fresh flowers and pale green recycled ribbon.

❊ High-tech organic skin care: luxurious natural brands and makeup free of synthetic chemicals (see page 175).

❊ City-center ecohotels: minimalist and low impact.

❊ Biodynamic wines: Some of the world's top vineyards use this approach.

❊ Peace silk: a light, ethical fabric for a handmade gown.

❊ Fair-trade artisanal chocolate: for edible favors and cakes.

❊ Limited editions: Support local artists by choosing handmade decorations.

❊ Contemporary, ethical jewelry: from certified diamonds to local hardwood rings (see page 79).

❊ Recycled glass: jewelry made from luminous sea-glass beads, shaped by the ocean (see opposite page and page 80).

❊ Designer organic cakes: visually stunning, in any shape you can imagine.

❊ Bespoke bouquets: Use fair-trade flowers to complement your dress, or grow your own flowers and foliage (see page 143).

❊ Rented topiary: Add elegance with formal box balls or a cloud-pruned olive.

❊ Ecoregistry: from stylish, green designer names.

❊ Biofuel wedding cars: Or, go low-tech with bicycles.

Handmade weddings

A DIY wedding can be enormous fun to create. Homemade cakes, decorations, invites, and dresses can really personalize your day, while also saving you money. Relax in the knowledge that your wedding will be distinctive and perfectly you.

To ensure your DIY wedding is memorably stylish, coordinate your stationery, match your flowers to your dress details, and choose decorations that complement your venue.

Picture the scene: trees looped with homemade gingham bunting and tables laid with plates of home-cooked food and Grandma's chutney; pretty place cards, showing guests their seats, crafted out of recycled paper and reclaimed lace; a wedding gown made by the bride from a vintage pattern; flowers and herbs, planted into coir pots and small enamel jugs by a friend, and grouped as table displays. Perfect.

Family and friends

Depending on the size of your wedding, you may need an extra pair of hands to craft your day. Ask relatives to help out by making the cake or a plate of food. Or gather bridesmaids together for an evening of jewelry making. Invite a talented friend to take the photographs, and see if an older family member has a gown squirreled away that can be reworked into something wonderful.

Get your groom involved, and persuade him to make the chocolate truffle favors—easy to prepare and delicious. Pack them into biodegradable cellophane bags, tied with natural raffia, for wedding-day gifts. Spend time with friends creating your own recycled fabric corsages, and embellish a guest book using the same materials.

Handmade and bespoke

If hand-crafing isn't for you, or you are not confident of your skills, search out talented local artisans who can make everything from your dress to the bread.

Homemade tips

* Borrow books from the library to find out how to make invitations (see page 98).
* Find local courses in traditional printing techniques and jewelry making.
* Salvage charming old fabrics to make corsages, bunting, and tablecloths.
* Adopt "Ladies, a plate," a New Zealand tradition where female guests bring a dish of homemade food—ask all of the cooks among your guests, male and female to join in.
* Bake your own cupcakes and decorate them imaginatively (see page 127).
* Find a local dressmaker and have a gown made to measure—or, ask a friend or relative to make it for you (see page 62).
* Gather flowers from your garden and tie your own bouquet (see page 146).
* Make timber signs for the reception with your groom.

Your DIY wedding preparation kit

* Salvaged fabrics
* Recycled old ribbons and lace
* Antique printing kits
* Pebbles and beads
* Natural raffia
* Pinking shears and sharp scissors
* Handmade paper
* A sewing kit and sewing machine
* Plenty of time—and, of course, this book

Natural advantages

Lovingly handmade food, dresses, and decorations can reduce packaging and food miles, and DIY is an excellent thrifty choice.

Pawle and
Kiki,
love, laughter,
and happy times
4 ever ♡
lov,
Rachel + Martin
xx

Budgets and priorities

The budget can be a major influence on your day. But regardless of whether you have been saving for years or are strapped for cash, you can still have a glorious wedding. Don't be tempted to borrow money for your celebration—in my experience, this simply leads to stress and worry. It is better to start your married lives without this burden.

My advice to all couples at the beginning of the planning phase is to make a list of your wedding priorities. You may have your eye on a special designer dress or be desperate to invite two hundred guests, so working out what matters most to you is a good starting point.

Once you have your list, allocate the sums of money that you are prepared to spend on each item. Some wedding books and magazines suggest percentages for each, from the dress to the music. But if you follow this advice, you may end up spending more than you want on some things. Instead, simply divide up your budget according to your own priorities.

Being inventive

A natural wedding allows you to be resourceful and creative with your spending. If you decide to blow most of the budget on food, see if you can borrow a dress; or, if you simply cannot afford stationery, send out e-vites instead.

Don't be afraid to ask friends and relatives for their help and advice. They will often be happy to make food, provide bunches of flowers from their gardens, or lend pieces of jewelry or even a wedding dress. Make the most of their skills: Ask if they can style your hair, apply your makeup, or even teach you how to lino-cut your own invitations. They will almost certainly love to be involved.

Natural choices

You will probably have ideas about the one aspect of your wedding where it really matters to you to be as green and ethical as possible. Whether it is organic food, vintage collectables, ecofriendly products, or the perfect green venue, put this on your wedding priority list and remember to bear it in mind when searching out vendors.

It is easy to lose direction when planning a wedding and panic-buy things that you don't need and won't use. By re-reading your list and thinking about whether you really need a product, you can stick to your ethical principles and keep a rein on your budget.

For more planning help, see our Wedding Planner on page 202.

> **Wedding planner tip:**
> Add up your spending as you go along so you don't go over budget. Simple advice, but surprisingly effective.

Your ceremony

The ceremony is the keystone of your wedding and will define your day. There are many different ways to wed, whether you dream of a traditional church service or an alternative ritual, prefer a civil route or decide to "marry" without any official, legal ceremony. Rules and regulations differ in every country, so check with your local authority about what constitutes a legal marriage in your area. There are meaningful ceremonies for couples of all faiths; this quick guide will get you started.

Legalities

The requirements for a legal marriage vary from country to country and can be confusing. In the United Kingdom, you can be legally married in a church or other religious building, in a council registry office, or at a registered venue by a registrar. Outdoor marriages are more difficult and are only currently legal for humanists in Scotland. To marry legally outdoors in England, Ireland, or Wales the ceremony must take place under a registered shelter, usually on the grounds of a stately home or hotel.

Humanist weddings

In Scotland, Australia, New Zealand, Canada, Norway, and some states in the United States, humanist weddings are legal. These are nonreligious weddings where couples are encouraged to write their own vows and choose their own music and readings. Ceremonies must be conducted by a registered celebrant but can take place at any location as long as it is "safe and dignified." Whether under a blossoming tree or on a deserted beach, the possibilities for a humanist wedding are truly special.

Gay and lesbian weddings

The laws vary across the globe. In the United Kingdom, civil partnerships (for gay and lesbian couples) are legal in council registry offices and some registered venues. Other countries, such as the United States, allow civil partnerships in certain states, while some do not allow same-sex weddings at all. Any couple can choose to have a nonlegal commitment ceremony—you could even have a friend conduct the wedding.

Hand-fastings

A hand-fasting is an ancient pagan ceremony popular in many countries. During the ceremony, the couple's hands are tied together with a piece of ribbon, fabric, or cord, which when knotted, signifies that the couple's union is permanent. (This is where the saying "tying the knot" originates.) Hand-fastings are usually held in woodland with guests standing in a circle marked with stones. They are beautiful ceremonies and can be combined with a civil wedding for a legal marriage.

It's your day

Unless you are having a formal religious service, generally you can have some input into the design of the ceremony. Personalize your day by writing your own wedding vows and choosing readings, poetry, and music that are special to you both.

Ecophotography

It's simple to be green with your photos—just go digital. Ask your photographer to provide the images on a CD so that you can view and print them as you wish. Traditional photo-printing techniques use synthetic chemicals, so instead, print onto recycled paper using vegetable-based inks—see the Directory for specialist printers.

Wedding albums often have tropical hardwood covers that are sourced from Australia and New Zealand. If you live in the United States, the carbon footprint of the album alone is huge. Choose a company that provides locally produced, handmade paper albums with sustainably sourced timber covers. Old-fashioned, self-adhesive photo corners are preferable to spray glue.

Your wedding notebook—save cuttings, business cards, fabrics, and pictures showing ideas you like into a book to help you design your day.

A DATE TO REMEMBER

Celastrina argiolus

7 ♥

Holly Blue
23-30mm

Bath Organic Blooms at
The Walled Garden

BathOrganicBlooms

Farther afield and precelebrations

If you plan to marry abroad, with a little thought, it is still possible to have an ecofriendly wedding. A diverse and growing range of ecohotels and lodges across the world use organic food and local suppliers, have recycling strategies and green electricity tariffs, and promote fair trade. For peace of mind, ask the same questions you would of a venue closer to home (see page 38).

Think about how you intend to get there—traveling by train is better for the environment than flying—and consider offsetting your journey through accredited organizations such as www.carbonfootprint.com.

The legalities of marrying abroad vary from country to country. Most will require you to be "resident" for anything from a couple of days to a few weeks. Be prepared to provide a bundle of paperwork, including

passports, birth certificates, and sometimes a letter from your consulate. Unless you both speak the local language, an interpreter is essential. Check with the country's consulate for specific requirements and advice.

Alternative bachelor and bachelorette parties
Bachelor and bachelorette parties are a long-standing wedding tradition. But why not try something a little different? Friends of mine held a joint bachelor/bachelorette minifestival in a field. They erected a tent and invited local bands and DJs to play. Guests camped for the whole weekend and brought food to share.

Cheap flights to typical party destinations create large carbon footprints, so stay closer to home and take public transportation or carpool. See the box above for more ideas.

Dare-to-be-different bachelor parties
* Outward Bound weekends
* Survival courses
* Mountaineering trips
* Hiking expeditions

Fashionable bachelorette parties
* Crafting weekends
* Spa breaks
* "Glamping"—or, glamorous camping
* Home cocktail parties, complete with a professional mixologist

---

Packing tips for the bride abroad

Transporting a wedding dress can be a challenge. Follow these tips for stress-free packing.

* Choose a dress in a fabric that will not crease easily, such as silk.

* A shorter dress or skirt-suit is much easier to transport than a long gown.

* Place layers of acid-free tissue paper between the folds of your gown to minimize creasing.

* Vintage dresses often travel more happily than you would expect, as the beading and lace can disguise wrinkles.

* Small, beaded vintage purses make a stylish alternative to a bouquet and take up minimal space.

Wedding planner tip:
Expensive precelebrations can be too costly for some friends. More affordable activities will make it easier for them to join in.

* **What makes a venue green**
  The essential questions to ask

* **Ecohotels and centers**
  From boutique hotels to organic
  bed-and-breakfasts

* **Weddings under canvas**
  Yurts, tepees, and traditional cruck marquees

* **Heritage and historic buildings**
  From romantic castles to working mills

* **The great outdoors**
  Beaches, arboretums, and wildlife centers

* **Going local**
  Neighborhood halls, friends' gardens, and top
  tips on rentals

* **Chair decoration**
  Easy and stylish transformation

The Venue

Choosing your wedding venue will be one of your
first and biggest decisions, so you'll want it to reflect
your values as a couple. There are plenty of charity,
thrifty, and naturally luxurious alternatives to the
standard hotel wedding package (even though some
chains are trying to be more ecofriendly). You can
hold your reception, and sometimes marry, anywhere
from a yurt in a friend's garden to an ecochic
boutique hotel or sumptuous historic house.

What makes a venue green

There is a stylish green venue for every celebration, whatever your beliefs or religion. The best way to find a venue is by personal recommendation, but guides and Web sites can also help. Some use questionnaires to determine the efforts that venues are making to be ethical and environmentally friendly; others, such as www.ecohotelsoftheworld.com, vet entries.

The questions below will help you to establish a venue's environmental credentials. You may have your eye on a fantastic place that doesn't fulfill all of these criteria, but some effort is better than none. It is up to you to decide what matters most to you.

Questions to ask a venue

❁ Does it have a recycling and waste management strategy?

❁ Does its energy come from a green energy provider, or does the venue generate its own electricity through on-site renewables, such as solar panels?

❁ Do the managers use local suppliers when possible?

❁ Do they choose fair-trade products?

❁ Do they opt for organic food, and is it grown on-site or locally?

❁ Do they clean using products that are free from petroleum-based and synthetic chemicals?

Energy use

Many buildings, from farms to modern hotels, now generate their own electricity. Greener venues may have a biomass boiler or a wind turbine, solar thermal panels, or photovoltaics. If not, they should at least buy their energy from a green provider.

Waste strategy

These days, there is little excuse not to recycle, and food waste is easily composted. However, some venues will go further in reducing, reusing, and recycling. Winkworth Farm in Wiltshire, England, for example, bottles its own water and reuses the glass bottles.

Reducing chemical exposure

Many people are now aware of chemicals such as volatile organic compounds (VOCs) that can affect health. Look for venues that decorate using natural paints and water-based varnishes; use gentle, nonsynthetic cleaning products; and have chosen furnishings that are made using natural materials or meet strict ecostandards, such as the Nordic Swan ecolabel.

Organic food and products

As well as cooking you a delicious organic wedding breakfast, venues can offer many other organic options, such as organic cotton bedding (regular cotton uses a quarter of the world's pesticides), organic bamboo towels, organic plant-wax candles, and organic toiletries. For more about organics and certification, see page 110.

Air-conditioning

Air-handling units (AHUs) use massive amounts of energy and also cause noise pollution. Even in hot and humid conditions, well-designed venues can cool their buildings naturally though windows and roof vents. If there is air-conditioning, make sure it is powered by renewable energy.

These "giant hat" Kåta tents can be joined in combinations to make different-sized spaces, from www.papakata.co.uk.

Before you start your venue search, it is useful to determine some basic criteria:

❊ Would you like to marry and hold the reception in the same location?

❊ Do you need a venue licensed for marriages? (Not required for hand-fastings or blessings.)

❊ How many guests do you plan to invite?

❊ Do you want the ceremony or reception to be indoors or outdoors?

❊ What time of year do you wish to marry?

Consider how your venue fits with your vision. If you are planning a formal affair with floor-length gowns and a lavish sit-down meal, a grand historic venue would be ideal. With an ecofabric dress, flowers in your hair, and a barbecue, a tepee in a field may be just right.

For more about legalities and licensing, see page 30. If you are marrying abroad, see page 35.

Wedding venue ideas

❊ 10 guests: ceremony in a tiny church, followed by a garden party in a friend's flower-filled garden

❊ 50 guests: civil ceremony and sit-down dinner at an ecoboutique hotel

❊ 100 guests: civil ceremony at a licensed, organic ecocenter, followed by an outdoor cocktail reception

❊ 200 guests: festival-inspired hand-fasting under a tree, followed by a reception in a giant tepee

Wedding planner tip:
To minimize guest miles and keep your wedding carbon footprint low, hold your ceremony and reception at the same venue.

From top: Penrhos Court, views
at Winkworth Farm, Dauntsey's
School, The Pump Room in Bath,
and Forever Green ecocenter.

Ecohotels and centers

Specialist green wedding venues can range from purpose-built ecocenters, constructed using locally sourced materials and sustainable building techniques, to carefully renovated buildings upgraded to the highest environmental standards. Often green venues will also grow their own food and flowers.

Ecovenues usually advertise their credentials, but if there is something specific that you are concerned about, do ask—they are generally happy to help. The Directory on page 208 lists some of our favorites.

Many hotels and ecocenters are licensed for civil ceremonies, while others may have chapels on their grounds, and some are set up to host the perfect hand-fasting (see page 30). Check which type of ceremony they can perform before you book the date.

Ecoboutique hotels

Often elegant town house conversions or innovative new buildings with holistic spas and contemporary interior design, these hotels score highly on the ecocredentials but do not compromise on luxury or comfort. Find ecohotels around the world at Organic Places to Stay (www.organicholidays.co.uk).

Organic hotels and bed-and-breakfasts

These tend to be smaller and more low-key than ecoboutique hotels. They aim to be as green, ethical, and sustainable as possible and use organic products— from soft, unbleached cotton sheets to organic shower gel. Ideal for more intimate weddings, some organic hotels have their own wildflower gardens or private beaches. Moss Grove Organic (www.mossgrove.com) in the Lake District was refurbished using clay paints, wool insulation, and reclaimed stained glass.

Sheepdrove Organic Farm
Berkshire, United Kingdom

Architect designed, with rammed-earth walls and a timber frame, Sheepdrove (www.sheepdrove.com), licensed for civil ceremonies, is a fine example of an ecocenter. The contemporary interior finishes include natural paints and recycled doors. All the food is organic and local, much of it grown on a 2,300-acre organic working farm—they even grow wheat for artisanal bread.

Specialist green wedding venues

Specifically designed or renovated to provide the ideal setting for a natural wedding, venues such as Sheepdrove (above) have the highest environmental standards. Some are entirely wind or solar powered. Most will provide all you need for your day, from locally grown flowers to organic food and their own free-range eggs. Keep an eye out for those that offer something different for your guests, such as a garden maze, a seawater pool, or a stone circle. Many are surrounded by beautiful, organic gardens—a wonderful setting for an idyllic wedding.

Wedding planner tip:
Think about how far your guests will need to travel to your wedding. Long journeys leave large carbon footprints.

Weddings under canvas

Holding a reception under canvas is an exciting prospect and a practical solution for couples with a large guest list but not the budget to match. Marquees, tepees, yurts, and Bedouin tents offer great opportunities for unusual and striking decorations, and an outdoor reception gives a relaxed, informal feeling to the day.

Fields and farms can provide the perfect setting. Often farmers will rent out a field for a day or weekend; some will even provide local produce. Ask if you can borrow straw bales for seating, and whether there are toilets nearby for your guests. Always check with the relevant authorities if you need either a tent or liquor license for the event, and make sure there is access for your tent rental company and any guests with disabilities. You can set up a small kitchen tent and rent catering equipment, although food prepared beforehand will mean less fuss. See page 116 for catering ideas, and the Directory for tent rental companies.

Tepees

Tepees and Kåta tents are hand-crafted timber pole structures covered with natural canvas. The design allows for easy assembly and is intended to include a real fire in the center. "Giant hat" Kåta tents are huge and can be joined together to form beautiful arrangements with enough space for hundreds of guests. Rental companies can provide gorgeously rustic trestle tables and benches, which you can decorate with foliage and candles. During chilly evenings, lay vintage woolen or sheepskin blankets across the benches.

Wedding planner tip:
Ask musical guests to bring instruments with them to play when the band finishes.

Bedouin tents

The traditional, intricate design and colorfully printed canvas of Bedouin tents makes them a stunning backdrop for a wedding. Rental companies can provide hand-painted wall panels, ceiling swags, and embroidered floor cushions, as well as furniture.

Yurts

Curvy and magical, a yurt is a wonderful alternative to a tent. These circular structures can be linked to form yurt villages, which can accommodate the largest wedding party. Separate yurts could have different functions, such as a "bar" or "chill-out" yurt. Choose low tables and floor cushions for a laid-back atmosphere.

Cruck marquees

These are a traditional English timber frame overlaid with natural cotton canvas. Ideal for smaller gatherings, they are usually open at the sides, so are best chosen in months when the risk of rain is low. The attractive structure is simply enhanced by pretty native flowers and flickering candlelight.

Traditional tents

Usually made from natural canvas, with scalloped pelmets and "big top" peaks, these are suited to colorful, homemade bunting and candy-stripe ribbons. I've helped couples keep to a tight budget with a tent by avoiding extras, such as linings and carpets, and renting trestle tables and chairs separately. With all of these tent options, always check what is included in the price.

Guest camping

Some venues offer camping. You could set up a small field of tepees or ask guests to bring their own tents.

Canvas tips

❋ Look for companies that use sustainably
   sourced timber for their structures.
❋ Some rental companies are carbon neutral
   and plant trees to offset their delivery miles.
❋ A timber dance floor will help your guests
   to find their dancing feet.
❋ Wind fresh ivy around timber supports
   for natural decoration.
❋ Lay blankets across straw bales for instant,
   comfortable seating.

A wood-framed
cruck marquee.

Heritage and historic buildings

It is possible to find remarkable, historic wedding venues that are also ethically sound. Many larger buildings cover their high maintenance costs by hosting weddings and celebrations, so your wedding is helping to preserve them. Old buildings, constructed using traditional techniques, generally contain less-embodied energy than their contemporary counterparts. However, drafty mansions are likely to use more power in their day-to-day running. Venues that have been sympathetically upgraded to high energy-saving standards give the best of both worlds.

Historic homes

Stately homes, and other historic houses, are often licensed for civil ceremonies, and many will oversee all the elements of your day, providing staff and sometimes their own wedding planner. Frequently they have outstanding grounds and gardens. Think about choosing a venue owned by a charity, such as the National Trust (www.nationaltrust.org.uk), which supports architectural conservation. Wakehurst Place in Sussex, managed by the Royal Botanic Gardens at Kew (www.kew.org), includes an arboretum and the Millennium Seed Bank, with all profits going to its plant conservation program.

Country house weddings

Country house parties, where you rent a whole grand house for a day or weekend (rather like renting a vacation cottage), have become highly fashionable. Generally, you will have the place to yourself and are responsible for arranging outside caterers, music, and flowers, but check individual venues to see what is included. Look for those venues that have been carefully restored using environmentally responsible techniques.

Castles and follies

Castles are the ideal backdrop for a fairy-tale wedding. Some can accommodate your guests overnight, which cuts down on travel. Others, such as Thornbury Castle (www.thornburycastle.co.uk), have their own herb gardens and vineyards, so serve their own produce.

Small and intimate, follies range from miniature country houses to classical temples. A few are licensed for civil ceremonies, such as the Red House at Painswick Rococo Garden in Gloucestershire, England (www. rococogarden.org.uk). Team a folly with a traditional tent on nearby grounds.

Mills and barns

Brimming with rustic charm, mills have often been sympathetically converted, and may have fully working waterwheels and flour stones (so you can serve homemade bread using their flour). Winkworth Farm mill (www.winkworthfarm.com) has solar-powered hot water and a cutting garden, too.

Barns can be small and unconverted, with straw on the floor, or grand architectural transformations. There are good examples to fit all budgets and sizes of weddings.

Church weddings

Ancient churches lit by candlelight can be one of the most romantic settings for wedding ceremonies. Fees vary, but all go toward the upkeep and maintenance of these historic buildings. Why not arrange to leave your flowers for the next service?

The grounds of Sheepdrove
Organic Farm in Berkshire.

Wedding planner tip:
Ask the owner of a park or garden if
you can pick a few flowers for your hair,
bouquet, or boutonnieres.

The great outdoors

For those who love being outdoors, there can be no better place to marry than in a garden or wood, or on a sandy beach. Riverbanks, arboretums, and lakeshores all make wonderful settings, while marrying under a beautiful, ancient tree is intimate and romantic, with little environmental impact. Inclement weather can pose a problem, so look for a venue with its own shelter, and select appropriate footwear.

For information on the legalities of marrying outdoors, see page 30.

Arboretums

Full of ancient trees, blossoming shrubs, and wildflowers, arboretums, for me, are perfect venues. Many are happy to host weddings and have small buildings available for year-round celebrations, often built using their own timber. Marry in springtime to take advantage of tree blossoms, or in autumn as the leaves change color.

Botanical gardens

What could be better than strolling with your guests through a colorful, wildlife-filled floral garden? Botanical gardens often incorporate streams and boating lakes, and some have their own follies, ideal for a ceremony. Check with the gardens (or the local authority) to find out whether they are licensed and allow weddings.

Local parks

You may have a park near your home that you visit throughout the seasons. Well-maintained and full of champion trees and specimen plants, parks can provide the ideal backdrop—not only for photographs but also for a wedding-party picnic. If you are marrying in a nearby church, why not host drinks in the park? You will need to ask permission from the local authority.

Wildlife conservation centers

These make unusual and inspirational settings. Wildlife charities work hard to protect endangered species and habitats and to rehabilitate animals of all types. You could link your wedding list to your chosen center and ask your guests to make a donation to their valuable work.

Beaches

A beach wedding party can be an ideal low-impact reception. With invigorating scenery, plenty of space for guests, and fabulous photo opportunities, you and your friends will love it. Check for water quality at www.blueflag.org, make sure there are bathrooms nearby, and always clean up thoroughly afterward. Ask the local authority before you plan your event: Some beaches allow campfires, but others have restrictions (on dogs, for example). You should also consider how your guests will travel to the beach, whether there are any hazards, and tide times (so you don't get stranded).

Going local

If you live in a house with a beautiful garden, or have friends or relatives who do, why go any farther for your wedding party? It's a thrifty option, and environmentally friendly, as you can recycle as much as you like, and guests may be able to walk there. Encourage those traveling longer distances to use public transportation or to carpool to reduce parking issues. You can easily obtain temporary tent licenses from your local authority—useful in case of rain. Remember to inform neighbors of your plans, to keep them happy, too. For more about setting up a garden party, see pages 23 and 159.

Finding a hall

Village halls and community centers are great for those on a tight budget. Many have on-site catering facilities and provide a blank canvas ready for inventive decoration. Don't worry if you are not keen on the furniture; simply rent different tables, chairs, and linen to personalize your day. Village halls are often positioned next to churches and chapels. At one village hall reception, we strung up floral bunting and laid a single flower on each napkin, and a couple of friends' sons acted as waiters and served the drinks.

Renting what you need

Practically everything you will ever need for a wedding is available to rent. Try to choose natural materials, such as wooden tables and linen tablecloths. Local companies will mean lower transport distances. Appoint a trustworthy friend to unpack deliveries and supervise collection.

> **Available to rent**
>
> Tables, chairs, cushions, blankets, tablecloths and napkins, crockery and glassware, cutlery, bars, candelabras, vases, cake stands, and cake knives.

Quick ways to transform your venue

With some imagination, it is possible to convert the plainest of venues into a wedding wonderland. Work with what is already there—not against it—for the best results. See the Directory for suppliers.

❈ Rent different furniture—choose trestle tables and benches to make best use of the space.

❈ Cover unsightly tables with tablecloths made from unbleached cotton, natural linen, or vintage fabrics.

❈ Use plant-wax candles and lanterns to light the room (check that they are allowed).

❈ Rent chair covers to disguise old chairs.

❈ Personalize the bathrooms by providing your own natural soaps and washes.

❈ Use flowers creatively to divert attention from less attractive elements.

❈ Put up small handmade signs to direct your guests.

❈ Use fabric drapes to cover unappealing wall features.

❈ Choose candles naturally scented with essential oils to make the room smell fresh.

❈ Bring your iPod for the music.

❈ Rent mismatched vintage plates for retro chic.

❈ When choosing flower decorations, complement or incorporate a color that is already in the room.

❈ Hang homemade bunting outside or inside to brighten up a dull color scheme.

Chair decoration

This decoration was made with fresh lavender, as it was in season at the time, though dried lavender also looks lovely. I find gingham ribbon works particularly well, but you could use whatever suits your style.

You can use these decorations for the bride and groom's chairs, or to show the seating places for close family. Alternatively, this type of decoration works beautifully for pew ends in a church.

FOR EACH CHAIR YOU WILL NEED:

45 lavender stems

3 ¼ feet of ¾-inch-wide gingham or other ribbon

12 inches of ½-inch-wide matching ribbon

Twine

Florist's shears or garden scissors

Fabric scissors

METHOD:

1. Take two lavender stems and cross one over the other just below the flower.
2. Cross a third stem over the second and repeat until you have fifteen stems, all crossed.
3. Put the bunch aside, and repeat steps 1 and 2 until you have three matching bunches.
4. Take one bunch and carefully add a second to the side. Add the third bunch.
5. Check the symmetry and make sure that all the stems are crossing one another in the same direction.
6. Pull some of the stems lower to create a fuller effect.
7. Tie the bunch together securely under the flowers with a short piece of twine. Knot, and trim the ends off the twine.
8. Checking the size of the decoration against your chosen chair, use the shears to cut the stems off the bunch so that they are level.
9. Place the thinner ribbon vertically behind the bunch and tie it on with the wider ribbon.
10. Wrap the wider ribbon around the bunch a couple of times and fasten into a bow.
11. Trim the ends of the wider ribbon into small Vs with fabric scissors, aligned with the bottoms of the stems.
12. Tie onto your chosen chair.

Wedding planner tip:
Instead of lavender, you could use dried sheaves of wheat for a rural feel or for a harvest-time wedding.

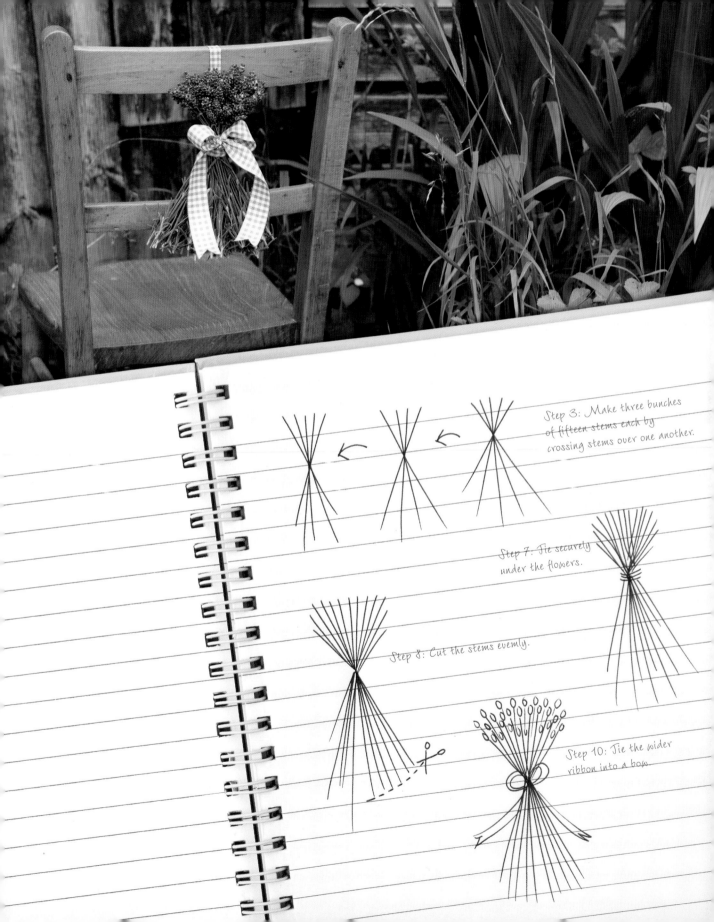

Step 3: Make three bunches of fifteen stems each by crossing stems over one another.

Step 7: Tie securely under the flowers.

Step 8: Cut the stems evenly.

Step 10: Tie the wider ribbon into a bow.

The Dress

The dress is probably the most important and exciting of all your wedding purchases, and what places you center stage. It is essential that you are comfortable in your choice, not only physically (you want to be able to breathe and sit down on your big day, but emotionally, too. This chapter suggests many fabulous, stylish, and unusual options, so relax, take your time, and enjoy finding your perfect gown.

Choosing your style

Step beyond the traditional shop-bought gowns and you'll find many exciting alternatives: svelte 1960s lace-covered shifts won on eBay; froths of chiffon from specialist vintage suppliers; gowns lovingly handmade in peace silk; floaty, organic cotton maxidresses worn with flower-woven hair; an heirloom gown reworked to fit perfectly; or a designer sample donated to a charity. All of them are special and they won't cost the Earth.

Most wedding books will tell you to start shopping with your budget figure in mind, but this may mean you end up spending exactly that amount and discounting other avenues because the dresses are below your budget. The easiest way to begin is by thinking about your wedding style and the season, and how you would like to feel on the day.

Your wedding notebook

Armed with your answers to the questions on the notepaper (below left), you should be able to focus more closely on your perfect dress type. At this stage, it is useful to keep a small notebook and to clip and paste any pictures, cards, fabric samples, or sketches that you feel could be useful when choosing a dress (see the wedding notebook on pages 32–33). Keep photos of flowers, venues, and accessories, too—they will all help to give you a feeling of your day and to enable you to choose a dress that will fit with your vision.

Starting with your dress

Your dress can influence the whole style of your wedding. So if you dream of an elegant, minimalist reception, look for simple, classic cuts. For an intimate city wedding for two, set off a film-star vintage pencil skirt–suit with a vibrant corsage. Think about colors, textures, fabrics, and shapes.

For a seasonally inspired look, you could choose your dress to complement your flowers—something delicate for cottage garden sweet peas or sumptuous velvet to go with winter blooms and rich foliage.

Natural options

Luckily, there are many different dress avenues open to you, from gorgeous ecofriendly fabrics to vintage dresses to die for. Feel free to mix it up! It's your day and your chance to shine.

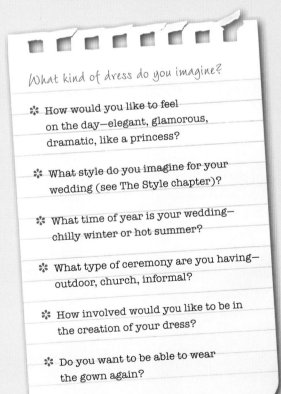

What kind of dress do you imagine?

❀ How would you like to feel on the day—elegant, glamorous, dramatic, like a princess?

❀ What style do you imagine for your wedding (see The Style chapter)?

❀ What time of year is your wedding—chilly winter or hot summer?

❀ What type of ceremony are you having—outdoor, church, informal?

❀ How involved would you like to be in the creation of your dress?

❀ Do you want to be able to wear the gown again?

Wedding planner tip:
Brilliant, pure white is a difficult color to wear. Ivory, cream, and ecru are generally more flattering.

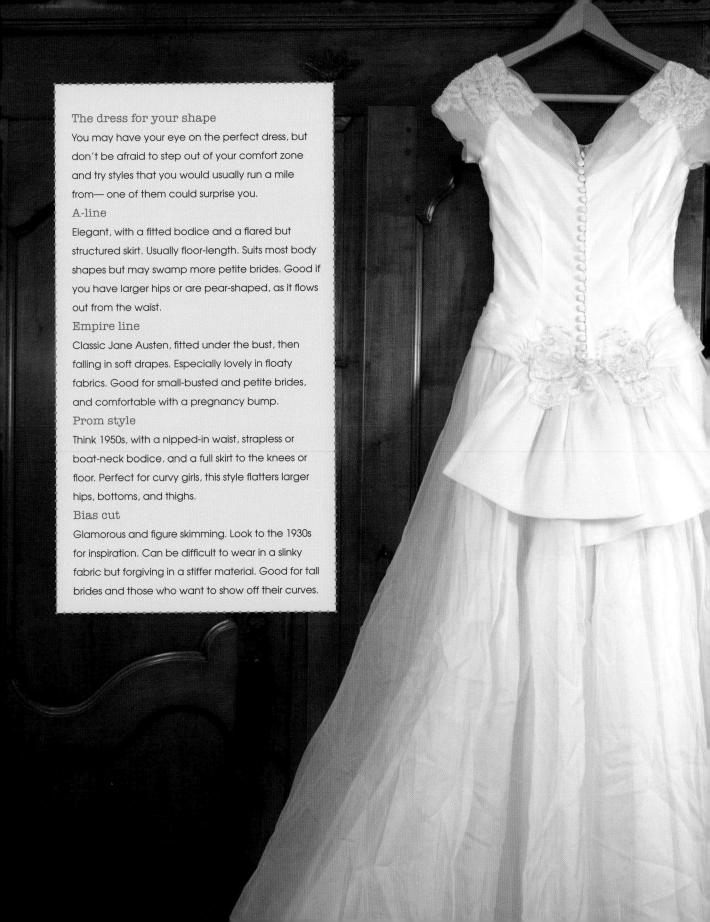

The dress for your shape

You may have your eye on the perfect dress, but don't be afraid to step out of your comfort zone and try styles that you would usually run a mile from— one of them could surprise you.

A-line

Elegant, with a fitted bodice and a flared but structured skirt. Usually floor-length. Suits most body shapes but may swamp more petite brides. Good if you have larger hips or are pear-shaped, as it flows out from the waist.

Empire line

Classic Jane Austen, fitted under the bust, then falling in soft drapes. Especially lovely in floaty fabrics. Good for small-busted and petite brides, and comfortable with a pregnancy bump.

Prom style

Think 1950s, with a nipped-in waist, strapless or boat-neck bodice, and a full skirt to the knees or floor. Perfect for curvy girls, this style flatters larger hips, bottoms, and thighs.

Bias cut

Glamorous and figure skimming. Look to the 1930s for inspiration. Can be difficult to wear in a slinky fabric but forgiving in a stiffer material. Good for tall brides and those who want to show off their curves.

Vintage gowns

Vintage, heirloom, and secondhand dresses (sometimes known as "preloved" or "loved for longer") are perfect for women who, like me, enjoy rummaging in antique and thrift stores. They can be altered or embellished to suit your body shape and personality, and they are often one of a kind. Strictly speaking, vintage covers the 1920s to 1960s, with pre-1920s classed as antique and 1970s onward as retro.

The dress Sophie is wearing in the top picture on page 58 is an early 1960s cream-colored lace shift with an elegant high neck, which I bought a few years ago on eBay, simply because I fell in love with it. The dress cost less than forty dollars, including shipping, and arrived boxed, in perfect condition, complete with details of its happy history.

Where to buy

❋ Specialist vintage clothing shops and fairs in your area
❋ eBay and other online auctions
❋ Markets
❋ Garage and trunk sales (you would be amazed!)
❋ Web sites such as www.freudianslipsvintage.com (see the Directory for more)

Buying a vintage dress

Specialist vintage shops can give invaluable advice. An expert can tell you if a dress will be easy to alter or too fragile to dance in. He or she should also be able to date your find and may even offer insight into its history. Bear in mind that you do pay a premium for this level of service. While it's possible to find good vintage dresses for next to nothing, rare examples can cost the same as, or even more than, a new designer dress.

Get to know the shops you are visiting, as prices will vary. Research your subject so you know what you are looking at and the likely value. It can be helpful to take an honest (but open-minded) friend or relative—and remember that hems can be shortened and embellishments added to cover the odd imperfection. Vintage dress sizes come up about two sizes smaller than modern equivalents. This explains why, although Marilyn Monroe is reported to have been a size 14, her dresses look tiny. Browse the online dress racks at www.londonvintageweddingfair.co.uk for inspiration.

An alternative is secondhand modern dresses, which can be cheaper and in better condition. We found Lisa's pink dress on page 187 at the Frock Exchange in Bath.

Online tips

Good measuring is the secret to buying when you can't try on. Check the waist, hips, bust, shoulder width, overall length, and sleeve length. Then compare these with a dress that fits you well.

Ask questions of the seller: Does the zipper work? Are there any visible marks or moth holes? Does the dress have any odors? You can always ask for extra photographs.

Opting for certified delivery will help to ensure your gown arrives as promised.

Wedding planner tip:
Look online for wonderful vintage designer dress patterns—they cost a fraction of the price of a designer-label gown.

Decades of style

1920s: The flapper dress

Skirt lengths rose daringly high (for the time) and bodices were short sleeved or sleeveless. This was an age of elaborate decoration and fine fabrics: tiny glass beads and metallic threads combined with crepe de chine, satin, and taffeta.

1930s: Age of glamour

Slender waistlines, long skirts, and long sleeves, often in satin. The backless, bias-cut evening gown created a silhouette favoring slim hips and wider shoulders. Accessorized with boleros and small capes.

1940s: Wartime utility ▶

Dresses were well proportioned and made to last. Silk was banned during the war, as it was needed for parachutes. Embellishments included covered buttons and sequins, which were readily available.

1950s: Prom queens ▶

A nipped-in waist and big, circular skirt, preferably with a full underskirt. Bodices were usually strapless and worn with elegant, elbow-length gloves and strings of pearls.

1960s: The mini

This style was boyish, with straight-cut minishift dresses teamed with block heels and glossy patent leather. Decoration was minimal for the modern look.

1970s: Boho style ▶

After the geometric tailoring of the 1960s came the long, flowing lines of the maxidress, with extended angel or bell sleeves. A fluid, romantic look decorated with strings of beads and daisy appliqué.

1980s: Anything goes

Many different styles emerged, from punk to Victoriana, with wedding dress styles following high-street fashion. The quintessential 1980s dress had a full skirt and was heavily decorated with frills, ruffles, puff sleeves, and lace.

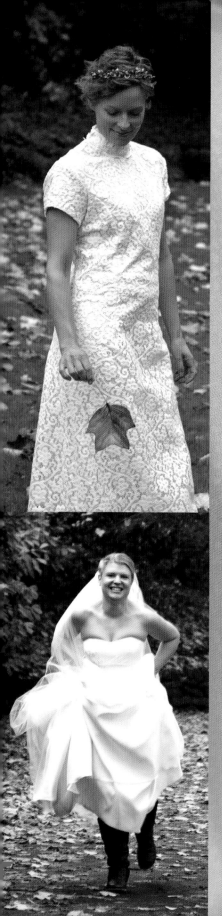

Charity chic

Charity shops have become increasingly popular in recent years, as fashionable celebrities frequent their local branches, looking for treasures. This new awareness has brought more competition for bargains, but it also means there is a wider choice of donations, including higher-priced items. Most thrift stores will stock wedding dresses from time to time, but it's worth visiting often, as stock may change daily. Ask friendly sales assistants if they can let you know when a wedding dress has come in.

Designer samples

The same rules apply to charity shopping as to vintage shopping, but if you have qualms about a secondhand dress, you'll be pleased to hear that many gowns donated to larger charities are either unworn, end-of-season stock, or runway samples given by designers. The dress pictured on the bottom left of this page still had its tags, and it was a fraction of the price it would have been in a designer shop. Reusing a dress or accessory is the ultimate in recycling, and it will help your budget, too.

Charity shops are also an Aladdin's cave of affordable accessories: everything from sparkly brooches and beaded tiaras to pretty vintage wraps and shoes. After the wedding, you can always donate items back to the shop.

Oxfam Bridal

Oxfam has a number of specialist bridal departments in the United Kingdom, stocking hundreds of fabulous dresses. Their prices will please the thriftiest of brides-to-be, and with the proceeds going to charity, it really is the most ethical choice. These bridal departments also stock jewelry, shoes, veils, bridesmaids' dresses, ring bearers' suits and flower girls' dresses, and menswear. With huge mirrors, generous fitting rooms, and a relaxed, friendly staff, you will not only have fun but likely also find a dress to impress.

My charity shopping tips

* Try to be open-minded and prepared to wait. You may discover the dress of your dreams on your first visit, but you may have to return several times to spot new arrivals.
* If you find a dress that seems perfect but is too big, don't despair. Most dresses can be altered to fit. If in doubt, ask the assistant to reserve the dress for you, and go back with an experienced seamstress to advise on alterations.
* Chances are there will only be one of each dress style, so if you fall in love with a gown, either buy or reserve it straightaway.
* Charity shopping, like vintage shopping, is all about being unique. So dare to be different, accessorize with flair, and be yourself.

What to take with you

❋ Your wedding notebook with inspirational pictures

❋ Camera (charity shops don't mind if you take photos)

❋ A pair of natural-colored tights

❋ A hair clip or hair band to tie up your hair

❋ Shoes of the height you want to wear on your big day

❋ A good friend to help you in the changing room

❋ Plenty of time

All of these dresses came from eBay and our local Oxfam Bridal. We took them to the park, and had some fun trying them on.

This hand-finished dress
by Jessica Charleston
is made from fine
natural silk.

New dresses

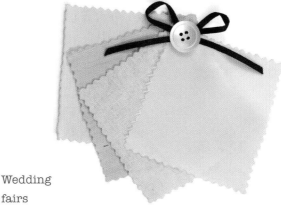

When buying new, there are, fortunately, now many designer brands that take ethics and the environment seriously. We love these labels and have listed some in the Directory. You could also try www.greenunion.co.uk or www.ethicaljunction.org. Garments made in good, humanitarian conditions tend to cost more, but you can find beautiful fair-trade silk and cotton gowns you will love.

Tammam, for example, uses organic and fair-trade materials, peace silks, and vintage trimmings, and sells off-the-rack as well as custom-made gowns. Alternatively, find a maxidress or a suit from an ethical designer, through ethical shopping sites such as www.ascensiononline .com, and add wedding touches with your accessories. Or try the amazing, deconstructed garments at www .junkystyling.co.uk, where you can take your old dresses to be reworked into something unique. Also check the guide to ecofriendly fabrics on page 64.

Shopping ethically

Not all bridal shops advertise where their dresses are made or the conditions for workers there. Some mainstream brands are manufactured in China and left chunky carbon footprints.

Many companies understand it is not acceptable to use child labor or pay below a minimum wage, and are making efforts to source their clothes more ethically, but unfortunately bad practices still exist. It is sometimes argued that developing countries need the employment provided by Western economies, but some employees are expected to endure unacceptable conditions, and communities may be exposed to toxic substances, such as the pesticides used to grow fiber crops, as a result.

My advice would be to ask where a garment has been manufactured. If you are keen on a particular brand, ask to see their ethics statement.

Wedding fairs

People often dismiss wedding fairs, but they can be a great place to discover small, family-run companies that manufacture locally, and up-and-coming designers of dresses, accessories, and wedding decorations who use natural and vintage materials. Many designers will sell their samples or discontinued stock and may offer a special exhibition discount. If you are prepared to decide on the spot, you could save a small fortune. Go wearing neutral underwear, pack your notebook, and take your mom or a friend. It can be a bit of a madhouse, so try not to impulse buy because you feel pressured.

Bridal shops

Some bridal shops are wonderful, will expertly fit a sample dress to your frame, and help you to choose the perfect accessories and bridal underwear to complete the picture. Others, however, will dictate which dresses you are "allowed" to try, tut under their breath, and generally make you feel uncomfortable. If you are looking for an ethical dress or natural fabrics such as silk, do ask questions, and feel free to visit and try on a dress more than once. Ask how many fittings are required and say when you would like the final one. There may be charges for delivery and storage.

Wedding planner tip:
I always recommend that brides sit down in a dress they are trying. Is it still comfortable?

Handmade and homemade

A handmade dress is a wonderful luxury when it's thoughtfully designed and made to fit you perfectly. Think about choosing an eco- or vintage fabric (see page 64). Handmade doesn't have to be expensive. Making your own wedding gown is completely possible if you have good sewing skills and the time. A reasonably simple pattern will be less stressful. Or you could ask a friend or relative—although, remember that you may have to request alterations if there are details you don't like, and you may find this awkward. The main cost will be the fabric, which can prove to be expensive.

If your ideal dress is elaborate, then a specialist dressmaker may be the wisest choice. Whichever route you decide on, have your wedding notebook on hand, with pictures, samples of fabric and other inspirations, to make sure that everyone understands your vision of the dream dress.

Home sewing

Before buying your pattern, it helps to try on ready-made dresses in differing styles so that you know what suits you. With your pattern, first make up a model in a cheaper fabric, such as natural calico (or an old bed sheet), so that you can adjust the fit and details.

Alternatively, use a dress that you love from your closet as a template. You will have to cut your own pattern, but this is not difficult, and most sewing classes can teach you how. Alternatively, a good dressmaker could do this for you. For hints and tips on all things sewing, www.burdastyle.com is the Web site to visit.

Vintage patterns

These are available through the same outlets as vintage dresses (see the Directory); patterns are inexpensive and easily customized.

Before you buy a vintage pattern:
❄ Check that all parts of the pattern are included.
❄ If the pattern has already been cut (not necessarily a problem), make sure it has been cut to your size or larger.
❄ Double-check measurements, not just the dress size, as vintage sizes are smaller.

Tips for working with a dressmaker

❋ A wedding dress is incredibly personal, so it is important that you click with your dressmaker. Choose someone through a recommendation and meet in person before committing.

❋ As with any professional, ask for a detailed written quotation and time estimate, follow-up references or testimonials, and a receipt for any deposits you pay.

❋ Study photographs and samples of the person's handiwork to check the workmanship on details such as seams.

❋ If you have a particular ecofabric in mind, or want only natural or vintage embellishments, ensure he or she is agreeable to this approach.

❋ A good dressmaker will be able to advise you on what styles will flatter your body shape, so listen to his or her opinion.

❋ If you don't like something about the dress as it is progressing, tell your dressmaker. Dressmakers are not mind readers, but they do want you to love your dress.

The Makery is one of the new breed of craft workshop, where you can have fun learning new sewing skills (www.themakeryonline.co.uk).

Ecofabrics

Designers and producers are bringing us a growing range of gorgeous fabrics that are gentler on our skin and on the environment. Many of these ecofabrics are a fresh twist on long-loved natural fibers. For suppliers see the Directory on page 208.

Peace silk (vegetarian or wild-crafted silk)

Silk is a completely natural product made from the cocoon of the silkworm. It is wonderfully light and breathable. However, traditional silk is harvested by boiling the cocoons and killing the worms before they hatch, which may offend some people.

When a silkworm hatches, it makes a hole in the end of the cocoon, breaking the continuous silk thread. With peace silk, the worms are allowed to hatch, and the fabric is made with the cocoon remnants. The resulting material is slightly rougher than regular silk but still beautiful. It is rarer and more expensive.

Hemp and hemp silk

Hemp is a relatively new material for wedding dresses, although it has been used in everyday clothing for many years. Environmentally friendly, hemp cloth is soft to the touch, although it has a slightly grainy appearance. It is often blended with silk to make a soft-sheen, satiny fabric that is lovely for special lingerie. Hemp grows quickly and easily, even in wet climates, and doesn't require fertilizers or spraying with insecticides.

Bamboo

Bamboo is a soft and smooth natural fabric that drapes well, almost like silk. Bamboo grass doesn't require fertilizers, grows quickly, and absorbs vast amounts of carbon dioxide. The fabric does not wrinkle easily, has natural antibacterial properties, and is a safer option for sensitive skins. Natural organic, unbleached bamboo is a flattering creamy color.

Organic cotton

Cotton is often overlooked as a celebration dress fabric, but it can be gorgeous when stitched with lace, and it is light and cool in summer. Most cotton is heavily sprayed with pesticides, so choose organic and fair trade when possible. For pure whites, look for ecobleached cotton.

Linen

You probably already have some linen in your wardrobe. Made from the flax plant, it is fairly labor-intensive to process, hence its high price. Linen is a great choice for summer, as it is so cool to wear, but beware of the dreaded linen wrinkles.

Nettle

Some may balk at the thought of using stinging nettles for their wedding dress, but they make a fabulous fabric with a slightly silky feeling. The fiber is often blended with organic cotton. Nettles are environmentally friendly plants, growing abundantly in damp, temperate climates.

Natural dyes

Modern, natural vegetable dyes, and instructions on getting the best results from them, are available online. You can transform any of the ecofabrics mentioned here to a color of your choice: Either dye the whole dress or just one element of it, such as a sash or corsage. Vegetable dyes come in an exciting range of colors, but if you feel unsure about dying the fabric yourself, buy it already dyed. For more information, look at www.greenfibres.com.

Vintage and reclaimed materials

A handmade dress in a vintage fabric will give you a gown that's unique and with a low carbon footprint, as the material has already been used once. You may have a trunk of fabrics and trimmings in your attic, but if not, you can find these in thrift stores, vintage costume stores, and online. You could also use material from an existing wedding dress—great if you have an heirloom or eBay dress and adore the fabric but not the style.

Think about remnants from fabric stores, too: There is minimal expenditure, and you're making use of a resource that might otherwise have been thrown away.

But remember that a wedding gown uses considerably more material than a regular dress. Embellishments such as ribbons, buttons, and bows can all be given a fresh lease on life as part of a new gown.

Wedding planner tip:
Use a vintage dress pattern with a contemporary ecofabric for a chic, individual look.

Dresses for free and cleaning

A free wedding dress? The idea will probably come as a surprise to most brides, but searching for a free dress can turn into an exciting challenge. Freecycle is a free-to-join online community where members post notices about unwanted items or ask for things they need. Do a search to find your local Freecycle or a similar community. You may get lucky and find an "OFFER: Wedding Dress," but you will almost certainly have to put up a "Wanted" post. Personalize this request, as the potential giver will want to know her special dress is destined for a good home. Freecycle is full of wonderful people, but like all online resources, it can be victim to the occasional bad penny, so be sensible when going to collect.

Something borrowed

"Swishing" parties have become something of a craze. Essentially, they are clothes-swapping events, to which you take your lovely-but-no-longer-worn items to give away in hopes of bagging a few choice pieces to revive your wardrobe. You are unlikely to find the wedding dress of your dreams, but may discover the perfect accessory, or even a white day dress or beaded evening gown.

How about borrowing from a friend? Most brides keep their dress for a couple of years at least. Don't let age fool you, either: Your mom's best friend may have the perfect vintage dress hiding in her closet. Check that it fits and that the owner doesn't mind if you make alterations.

Heirloom gowns

You may be the lucky inheritor of an heirloom wedding dress, passed down from your mother or even your grandmother. Don't discount it because it is not your style. Most dresses, even 1980s meringues, can be reworked, although you may need a seamstress. Alternatively, just reclaim the fabric and trimmings.

To rent or not to rent

New gowns that would cost thousands of dollars can be rented for a fraction of the price, and the fact that a rented dress is worn a number of times makes it a potentially ecofriendly option. However, the dresses will be dry-cleaned each time they are worn. If you have sensitive skin or are worried about the chemicals used, ask exactly how the shop cleans the dresses and if they use a more environmentally friendly cleaning process.

Cleaning and storage

Dresses should always be cleaned immediately after wearing and before being stored, as any perspiration on a dress discolors over time. While some modern dresses are machine or hand washable, others are dry-clean only, especially if they have beading or decorative elements. If a vintage gown looks clean but smells musty, hang it in a steamy bathroom for a couple of days. The steam will remove odors and help any creases to drop out.

Some specialists can dry-clean your dress without the toxic chemicals used in regular dry-cleaning. One option is called the GreenEarth process (www.greenearthcleaning.com). This is becoming increasingly widespread. These dry-cleaners are also the best places to buy an acid-free box and tissue in which to store your precious gown (remember to pad out the bodice with tissue if it is boned).

Covering stains

If stains refuse to disappear, you can always cover them up. First try a little chalk. This is a good emergency trick for marks discovered on the big day, and it will cover a blemish on most shades of white. Or hide the mark with an accessory, such as a corsage or brooch. No one will ever know! See the box on the opposite page for more ideas to add a fresh spark or personalize your dress.

Revive that dress

❋ Simply tie a wide satin ribbon in a contrasting color at the waist as a sash. Choose a hue to match your flowers, such as cornflower blue or velvety purple tulip. Fasten with a sparkly, vintage brooch.

❋ Pin a large flower corsage at the collarbone. Corsages are easy to make, so you could have a girly day with your bridesmaids and create accessories for your wedding (see page 68).

❋ Remove 1980s puff sleeves and net underskirts to transform a retro dress into a simpler, sleeveless silhouette.

❋ Shorten a dress that is too long and use the extra fabric to make a matching wedding-day bag.

❋ If a dress you love is too short, consider lengthening it with a fabric in a matching color but contrasting texture, or be daring and add fabric in a complementary color.

Emma's dress is a simple beaded 1920s-style chiffon. We added a vintage dress clip and drop earrings, and a corsage to match her coloring.

Fabric flower corsage

This corsage is easy to make in about an hour. You can use as many layers of fabric as you wish—the more layers, the more elaborate the finished corsage will be. For those shown in the photograph on the opposite page, I used a vintage silk slip combined with organic cotton.

YOU WILL NEED:

Natural fabrics such as silk, hemp, or organic cotton

Reclaimed netting from underskirts

Fabric scissors

Needle, pins, and matching thread

Piece of paper

Vintage buttons or a vintage brooch

Brooch backing

METHOD:

1. Cut a circle of fabric 4 inches in diameter, another in a different fabric 3½ inches in diameter, and a third 2½ inches in diameter. Cut two circles of netting, one 3½ inches in diameter and one 2½ inches in diameter.

2. Take the larger of the two fabric circles and place the larger netting circle on top of it. Secure together with a small stitch in the center.

3. On a paper measuring 4 x 2 inches, draw the shape shown on the opposite page, and cut out.

4. Cut out a rectangle of fabric 4 x 4 inches, and fold in half. Pin on the paper template and cut it out of the fabric. If using silk, after cutting, gently pull the edges at a diagonal, for a fluted effect. Make four more of these shapes.

5. Fold each fabric shape diagonally across once, then again, to make a "quarter." The edges should *not* line up.

6. Take two of the quarters and overlap them slightly, securing them with three small stitches. Overlap the other two quarters similarly; stitch to secure.

7. Place your "circle" of quarters in the center of your circle from step 2, then layer the remaining two fabric and net circles on top.

8. Position your button or brooch in the center and sew everything together.

9. Cut one final circle of fabric 1 inch in diameter. Take a brooch backing and sew this securely, through the tiny circle, onto the corsage.

10. Fluff up the petals, and enjoy.

Wedding planner tip:
These measurements are for the smaller corsage shown. To make a larger one, simply increase the sizes of fabric circles.

Step 4: Use the paper pattern to cut out your folded fabric.

This is the fabric shape you need to cut out.

Step 5: Fold your shape in half diagonally . . .

. . . and then again to make a "quarter."

Step 6: Overlap the quarters, and stitch.

Step 8: Layer your corsage and sew the button through.

Shoes, veils, and trains

It's often assumed that brides will wear white satin heels, but most of us don't have any use for this kind of shoe after the big day. How about silver or gold sparkly sandals, or even flip-flops, instead? Or invest in two pairs (affordable if they come from a thrift store): the killer heels for the ceremony and a comfortable alternative for dancing. If you choose something you really like—not just to go with the dress—you'll be more likely to wear them again.

Embellishing shoes can be surprisingly enjoyable: Pin on corsages or brooches, or glue on beads and sequins to give a wedding lift (but remember that less is more with decorations). I once worked with a bride who wore a formal floor-length gown, but glimpsed beneath, when she lifted her skirt, were a pair of pretty white shoes with crisscrossing blue ribbons. She had carefully stitched on the ribbons to mimic ballet slippers, and tied them in a decorative bow. The ribbon was vintage, so it was her something old as well as her something blue—and it added an element of surprise to her traditional outfit.

Depending on the time of year and where you are marrying, I would also recommend taking along a pair of Wellies. You can then go striding around the lake for amazing photographs with your new husband.

Veils

Some brides cannot imagine their wedding outfit without a veil, while others dread the thought. It also depends on your dress—a gold, sparkly cocktail dress wouldn't take a veil, for example. The usual guideline is that veils look best with white, ivory, or cream. The question of veil length is a minefield, but a good rule of thumb is the longer the dress, the longer the veil.

If you are lucky enough to have inherited a veil from a family member, it would be lovely to include this heirloom in your day. You can also find vintage veils, and with a little patience, you can make your own. Veils that are too long can be easily shortened with a few basic sewing skills (or by a seamstress). Similarly, you can buy a plain veil and add panache by sewing on small glass beads or ribbons. This could take a few hours but it will save you a small fortune. Look at embroidery books—the older, the better—for unusual patterns; search on Amazon for ideas.

Tips for choosing a veil

* Consider your dress color, style, and length.
* Do you want to be able to remove the veil after the ceremony, or would you like to keep it on for the reception and dancing?
* Think about contrasting fabrics, such as lace.
* Are you going to be wearing your hair up or down?
* What time of year are you marrying? A veil can be quite a handful in gusty winds!

A quick word on trains

Generally speaking, the more formal the wedding, the longer the train—although, if you yearn to wear a gown with a ten-foot-long train on the beach, why not?

Make sure that you or a friend know how to bustle up the train (wedding speak for tying it up under the gown so you can dance without tripping over it). Long trains can be held off the floor with a thumb loop that hooks around your thumb or middle finger, allowing you to swish around elegantly.

Wedding planner tip:
Always break in new shoes before the wedding and scuff the soles to ensure comfy feet and no slipups on the day.

Grooms and bridesmaids

A groom can be adventurous, ethical, and ecochic—and enjoy being in the spotlight alongside his bride. It helps if your bride and groom outfits are in sync. With a groom in top hat and tails, the bride really needs a fabulous floor-length gown; but if you are wearing a short, silk shift dress, then he should be in a suit and tie. Think about coordinating the color of your bouquet or sash to his tie, cravat, or suit lining. You could even have fabrics or handkerchiefs dyed with natural vegetable dyes to match.

Natural fabrics

In summer, there's nothing more comfortable than a linen suit. Linen allows the skin to breathe, keeping the wearer cool. Remember it can crease, and looks better in a lighter color. Men's shirts can also be found in the natural fabrics listed on page 64. Hemp and organic cotton both look and feel great, and they are readily available.

Vintage groom

Your fiancé may have an heirloom suit hidden away, but if not, men's vintage shops are starting to spring up. Vintage or retro styles—think 1950s pinstripes and wide shoulders, or Sean Connery, slim-line 1960s suits—have become fashionable for grooms. As well as secondhand, you could also look at vintage-inspired styles, such as floral-patterned shirts.

Wedding planner tip:
Find ties, shoes, and cuff links in charity shops. Or, translate the tradition of wearing something borrowed to the groom.

Rented groomswear

Renting a suit is popular with grooms, as it's easy and costs less—especially with formal options such as morning dress. For a large wedding, with many ushers and groomsmen, renting is the perfect way to make sure the bridal party matches. If the groom wants to stand out, he could buy a colorful cravat, tie, or shirt to personalize his outfit. Pedro's outfit on page 187 is from www.mossbros.co.uk.

Splurging

Once in a while, a groom will have a suit custom-tailored for his big day. A lovely idea—and green, too—if the suit can be worn again. He could choose a lining in a bright color, perhaps one to match your sash or corsage. Why not opt for an ecofabric, such as linen, or an organic or vintage wool weave, and complement it with an unusual vintage lining.

Bridesmaids

Most of the advice in this chapter also applies to bridesmaids' outfits. For a formal wedding, the usual "rule" is that the bridesmaids should match the bride in some way, or, at least, one another. But if you are a free spirit, why not let your bridesmaids choose their own dresses?

I attended a wedding where the bridesmaids wore bright, floral, 1970s-style frocks not at all in keeping with the bride. But the overall look was amazing. If bridesmaids make their own choices, chances are they will wear their outfits again, making it more environmentally friendly.

With ring bearers and flower girls, the advice is simple: Make sure they are comfortable. For girls, ballet slippers are the best footwear. Flower girls like to have accessories, such as baskets of fresh flower petals, to make them feel special. Little boys are typically not fussy!

The Accessories

Choosing all the little bits and pieces to go with your dress—the bags and earrings and bracelets—can be such fun. Rummaging in vintage shops and antique markets with your friends; discovering artisan craftspeople and modern ecodesigners who'll craft something special. Personally, I can't resist searching for something unusual, and this chapter has plenty of ideas so you can find your dream accessories, too.

Creative places to find your jewelry

Shimmering sea-glass beads and intricate Victoriana earrings; heirloom gold bands; or sleek, modern minimalism—it's surprisingly easy to find a wealth of ecochic accessories, whatever your budget and personal style. There are plenty of alternatives, from online ethical stores to charity shops, recycling, borrowing, or making your own (see the Directory).

Take a picture of your dress or a cutting of the fabric with you to markets and shops, and remember Coco Chanel's advice: "When accessorizing, always take off the last thing you put on."

Heirloom finds

You may be lucky enough to have an heirloom piece from a relative. If it is faultless, you could wear it conventionally or think about imaginative ways to show it off. Pin a brooch onto a waistband, or use it as a hair accessory or to decorate a bag. Dress clips make fabulous shoe embellishments, and long necklaces can be wound around several times for a more modern feel.

If an item is damaged, don't rule out having it mended by your local jeweler or asking him or her to rework it into something more wearable. Stones can be salvaged and reused to make a completely different piece.

Antique gems

High-quality antique jewelry is an investment, but it often costs only a fraction of the price of a new piece and, being secondhand, is effectively carbon neutral.

You'll find geometric Art Deco rings, Edwardian marcasite brooches, Victoriana hat pins, and Georgian glass necklaces in specialist antique jewelry shops and markets, or at auctions by www.christies.com or www.bonhams.com—and they won't all cost a fortune. Online, browse www.alfiesantiques.com and www.steptoesantiques.co.uk. Pre-1940 jewelry is classed as antique, later as vintage.

Hallmarks on precious metals will tell you the quality of the piece, its age, and where it was made. The Miller's antiques guides are helpful if you want to learn more.

Vintage costume jewelry

Vintage jewelry is one of my favorite things and is easily found in flea markets, antique fairs, and thrift stores. Try www.vintagefair.co.uk, www.manhattanvintage.com, or www.lovevintage.com.au, depending on where you live. Raid your grandmother's or mother's jewelry boxes (with their permission, of course); they may have beautiful necklaces or brooches squirreled away that will look fresh and modern when teamed with the right dress.

Charity shops

These can be a rich source of inexpensive accessories, especially if you are happy to revisit regularly to check for new donations. Styles range from long, wooden-bead necklaces to delicate silver chains, lucite bangles, 1950s clip-on earrings, and 1980s cocktail rings. Frequently, they will be in immaculate, unworn condition. But even if a piece is broken or dusty, you can have it cleaned and repaired for minimal cost—so if you love it, take it home. Buying from charity shops is ecofriendly and ethical, too.

Markets and trunk sales

These are good places to find more modern secondhand designs. Go early to catch the bargains, and remember that they will only have one of each item.

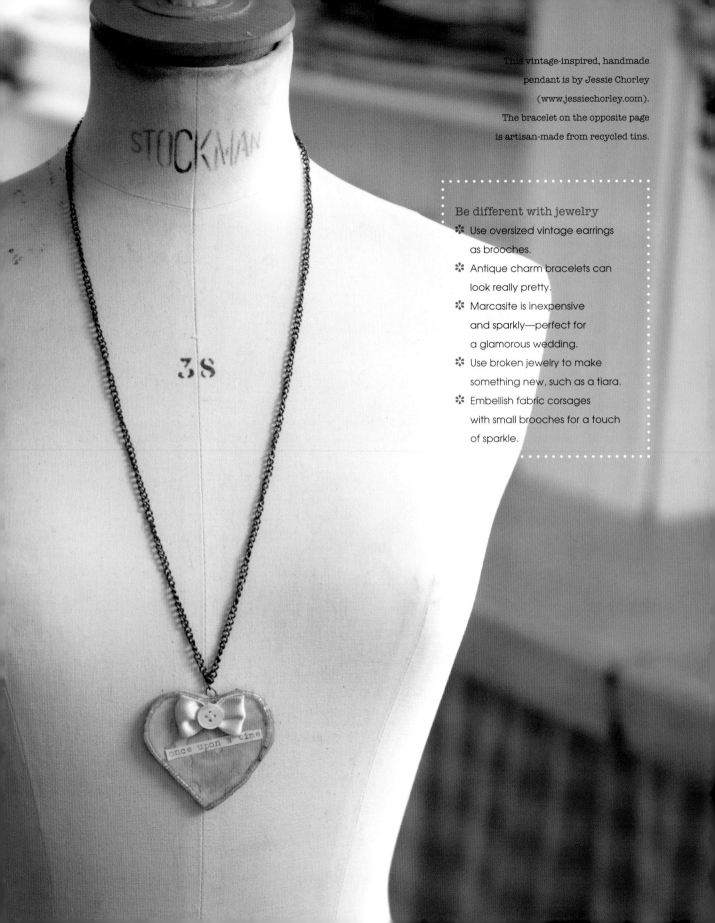

This vintage-inspired, handmade
pendant is by Jessie Chorley
(www.jessiechorley.com).
The bracelet on the opposite page
is artisan-made from recycled tins.

Be different with jewelry
* ❋ Use oversized vintage earrings as brooches.
* ❋ Antique charm bracelets can look really pretty.
* ❋ Marcasite is inexpensive and sparkly—perfect for a glamorous wedding.
* ❋ Use broken jewelry to make something new, such as a tiara.
* ❋ Embellish fabric corsages with small brooches for a touch of sparkle.

once upon a time

Ethical rings

The production of new gemstones can be damaging to the environment and sometimes the well-being of local communities, due to invasive and chemical-laden extraction techniques. Unethical working practices are commonplace. Responsible jewelry designers are now realizing that this is unacceptable and are reusing and recycling stones and metals when possible. You can also find beautiful fair-trade designs. See the Directory for jewelers we recommend.

Ethical diamonds

The issue of conflict (or blood) diamonds is now widely documented. Diamonds are still the preferred gem for engagement, wedding, and eternity rings, so it is important to do your research and buy with care. Nonconflict diamonds that have been mined and exported under fair-trade and ethical conditions are widely available. But the only way to be certain of where yours come from is to buy from a reputable dealer and check that he or she has certification. The Kimberley Process runs an international certification program for rough diamonds, helping to prevent the trade in conflict gems.

The Diamond Council also has a System of Warranties, whereby buyers and sellers of both rough and polished diamonds have to confirm that they are conflict-free and in compliance with United Nations' resolutions. See www.greenkarat.com and www.diamondfacts.org.

Unfortunately, all diamond mining—even ethical production in countries such as Canada—causes environmental damage, simply due to the process. Synthetic diamonds are becoming more popular as an alternative and are said to be indistinguishable from mined diamonds. Whether they are a suitable replacement for a naturally occurring mineral comes down to personal choice, although they are now considered to be the most ethically and environmentally conscious option. Browse online at www.greenkarat.com.

Cleaner gold and platinum

Gold and platinum extraction carries a high environmental price, since it uses chemicals such as mercury and cyanide. You can find cleaner gold and platinum, mined under better environmental and fair-trade conditions, although supply is currently limited. Ask your jeweler if he or she uses these cleaner metals.

Both gold and platinum are highly recyclable and can be reused to make rings and jewelry that appear new, with no further environmental impact. Look for artisans using postconsumer, recycled gold and platinum.

You may have a piece of jewelry at home that could be melted down and made into a new ring. Some jewelers will happily do this for you and encourage you to be involved in its design. A number of innovative companies hold workshops at their studios so that you can come in and help with the process of making the rings yourselves (see the Directory).

Wooden rings

These are a delightful, ethical alternative to metal rings and are skillfully crafted from native nontropical hardwoods, such as yew, oak, and cherry. Completely natural, and warm to wear, wooden rings will last for years with the correct care. They often come presented in a matching wooden box. The rings pictured above are from www.wooden.co.uk, or see www.etsy.com.

Wedding planner tip:
Clean gemstones using an old, soft toothbrush and eco-dishwashing liquid for sparkling results.

Beads for all occasions

*B*eads are always in fashion, whatever the season, and come in all manner of sizes, lengths, shapes, and styles (see the tips on the opposite page for ideas). They are easy to string yourself: Look for courses to learn beading techniques and to gather inspiration. Try salvaging broken necklaces and using the beads to create something new.

Sea glass

Fragments of glass are naturally polished by the sea into smooth pebbles in shades of blue and aqua, foamy white, rich green and amber, and, occasionally, rare pink. Sea glass can be hundreds of years old, and each piece is unique. Gina Cowen (www.seaglass.co.uk) makes magically beautiful sea jewels (see left and page 25).

Recycled beads

Look in galleries and online for inspiring artisan-designed, ecofriendly necklaces and bracelets made from recycled glass beads. Brilliantly reflective and found in countless colors, they make stunning jewelry (see www.juzionline.com).

Buttons

Pretty vintage and antique buttons with intricate designs can be used in the same ways as beads. Simply thread them onto fine beading string (available from craft suppliers) so the buttons lie flat. Search out antique mother-of-pearl buttons, which gently reflect the light. Find vintage buttons at charity shops (they are often cut off of damaged garments that are going to be recycled as textiles), online, and at specialist antique market stalls.

Beaded tiaras

These are easy to make—and a workshop can be a fantastic alternative bachelorette party. Use salvaged beads and recycled fine wire for a perfect ecoaccessory. It's worth checking frequently in a mirror to make sure that your design suits your face shape.

Hair bands and daisy chains

Hair bands add interest with minimal effort, whether your hair is long or short. Simple to make from elastic or wire, they can be wound with fine ribbons and decorated with vintage corsages, bows and brooches, or fresh flowers.

Narrow, fabric hair bands are especially chic worn across the forehead with loose, flowing hair—perfect for a laid-back beach wedding. Decorate with small, fabric blooms and tiny beads for natural summer style.

We made impromptu daisy chains for our bride, Lisa, above, and our flower girls—simple, beautifully effective, and ideal for an informal country or garden wedding. Remember to make them at the last moment so that they stay fresh.

Wedding planner tip:
The current trend is to wear either earrings or a necklace, but not both together.

Boleros and corsages

The accessories you choose can lift a plain dress or tie an outfit together. Try unusual combinations of color, textures, and layering, as we have in the photograph on the opposite page. Boleros and wraps can be useful whether your wedding is in deep winter or high summer.

Boleros, which are cropped, midsleeved jackets, are smart and stylish as part of a skirt-suit, or keep cold at bay when worn over a dress in the winter months.

Fine silk wraps will shield bare arms from hot sunshine or add a layer of warmth in early spring and autumn. Knitted ballet-wrap cardigans in creamy whites and soft pinks, finished with wide, satin ribbon ties, add a twist to a traditional strapless dress.

Scarves

I always feel that scarves are an underused wedding accessory, whether vintage silk or heavy knit. If your photographs are being taken in snow, a chunky, white bobble scarf will add fashion-shoot glamour.

Gorgeous old silk scarves from vintage shops come in all sorts of patterns, colors, and sizes. Larger ones can be used as a wrap, while the smaller ones look fabulous simply tied asymmetrically around the neck. This look is especially chic with a 1950s dress. You can even use men's brightly colored, silk hankies as scarves—vintage handkerchiefs are usually well made.

If you are having a dress made in an ecofabric such as hemp silk or raw peace silk, you could use the offcuts to make delicate scarves to match.

> Wedding planner tip:
> Update an existing wrap cardigan by swapping knitted ties for beautiful, reclaimed satin ribbons.

Ribbons

Vintage ribbons in unusual colors and textures can make strikingly simple accessories. For an almost instant choker, hem the ends and attach a small piece of Velcro or a button fastening to them. A friend made a contrasting black-and-white choker as a last-minute necklace alternative before heading out as a wedding guest. You could try layering ribbons in different widths and tones, or sewing on a corsage, beads, or buttons.

Corsages

Fresh-flower and fabric corsages are in vogue, worn with jeans as well as wedding dresses. You could make your own from cream-toned ecofabrics, handmade felt, or brightly colored offcuts of material (see page 68 for my simple method) or scout out vintage gems. If you find a fabric corsage that you adore but is in poor condition, give it a new lease on life by carefully taking it apart and reworking it, adding extra fabrics and ribbons.

Using fresh flowers

Floral accessories have a minimal carbon footprint if the flowers have been grown locally.

❋ Fresh-flower wrist corsages are the ultimate retro-prom accessory. They can look wonderful, especially for an outdoor wedding—and you could give your bridesmaids smaller matching versions.

❋ Try attaching a single fresh flower to one side of a ribbon sash. Ask advice from your florist as you will need a relatively hardy species.

❋ Floral headdresses have recently come back into fashion. They work best with tiny seasonal blooms that complement your skin tone and dress.

We want your
KITCHEN WASTE

PIG
FOOD

Soup!

Says 'POTATO PETE'

DOCTOR CARROT
the
Children's
best
friend

Ways with corsages
✻ Fasten a beautiful,
  antique corsage to
  a length of ribbon as a
  vintage-inspired choker.
✻ Wear a large fresh-flower
  corsage in your hair.
✻ Oversized, soft, ecofabric
  corsages look fabulous
  attached to matching
  wide belts for urban
  ecochic.
✻ Ask your dress designer
  for extra fabric to make
  your own corsage.
✻ Give your bridesmaids
  individual style with
  matching dresses but
  contrasting corsages.

This simple dress, shot at
the Makery, is lifted by a matching
1940s corsage and ballet wrap, and
a play-in-the-snow, chunky knit scarf.

Hemp-silk camisole from
Jenny Ambrose at Enamore.

Camisoles and pretty underwear

Beautiful underwear made from hemp silk and vintage ribbons are a fabulous indulgence for a bride. Ecogirls will love the soft, organic bamboo or natural cotton ranges that are now available, complete with pretty lace trimmings. Look online at makers such as www.enamore.co.uk. Choose fair trade for maximum ethical score, or make your own using vintage fabrics. Find easy patterns at www.burdastyle.com.

Perfect underwear

❋ Try your chosen underwear on with your dress, as sheer fabrics may reveal more than you bargained for.

❋ Ivory or nude-colored underwear is best under white, ivory, and champagne dresses. With a strong-colored dress, such as red, you could team your underwear accordingly.

❋ Splurge on some beautiful wedding-night lingerie in a light, ecofriendly hemp-silk mix.

❋ Lingerie workshops, where you can learn to make your own, are a new craze. Use organic, skin-friendly ecofabrics and vintage ribbons and lace to fashion something unique.

❋ Embellish your own favorite underwear with vintage, blue ribbons for your "something old" and "something blue."

Corsets

Amazing handcrafted corsets in modern ecofabrics will help to define your shape on the big day. These can be an extravagant purchase, but they are tailored to fit and will last for years if well made. Corset making is a skilled art with a finished piece taking many hours to complete. A design decorated with ribbons and lace will add a feminine touch. You will need to take details of your dress with you so the corsetiere can work to its shape.

Garters

Garters are a frivolous accessory that most brides will only wear on their big day but a traditional part of any wedding outfit. You can find handmade garters fashioned from salvaged lace and natural silk—and finished with a blue ribbon bow.

Having a Hepburn moment

Gloves can add a chic dimension to any wedding outfit—think of cult screen-icon Audrey Hepburn. They come in many lengths, from wrist to above the elbow, in a variety of fabrics to match or contrast with your dress. Pretty lace gloves work well with a delicate dress, heavier fabrics with more structured gowns.

Vintage gloves are usually beautifully made, readily available, and often cost only a few dollars from eBay and vintage specialists. Ensure that they are scrupulously clean, and remember that you will need to remove the left-hand glove during the exchange of rings, so make sure you can easily undo any buttons.

Think about dainty, knitted fingerless gloves, hand-embellished with tiny beads, for a winter wedding. You could team them with a delicate matching wrap or knitted choker. Gloves can also be useful for early spring or late autumn weddings. If you are wearing a cape, or a bolero or jacket with three-quarters-length sleeves, they will keep your arms warm.

Wedding planner tip:
Always hand wash silk and hemp-silk underwear to keep it looking its best, using a mild, plant-based detergent.

Bags of ideas

It is now perfectly acceptable for a bride (and her bridesmaids) to carry a small bag on the big day, sometimes in place of a bouquet. It can hold any items you may need, such as a hankie for those emotional moments or a lipstick for touch-ups. If you are making a speech, it's the perfect place to stash your notes.

You will find bags in the most unlikely places. I was browsing a stall that sold old tools at my favorite outdoor antiques market when I caught a glimpse of something sparkly—it turned out to be an apricot 1930s beaded bag, complete with an original vanity mirror. The stallholder told me that I could buy it for £5, and I still have it to this day.

You could also ask mothers and grandmothers, or try antique shops and trunk sales. Charity shops offer thrifty bags, some in as-new condition, from delicate satin clutches to modern, patent-leather purses.

Crafting your own

For those brides (or mothers) who are keen to make their own, try the instructions on page 88. This bag is quick and easy to make, and you can use pretty fabric remnants you may have at home or a new ecofabric (see page 64).

Embellish a bag

Even easier is to embellish a bag you already own. Adding a piece of vintage lace, a satin corsage, or a sparkly brooch can instantly transform a plain bag.

Top bag tips

❀ Enliven a simple dress with a decorative bag.
❀ Gold and silver bags double as jewelry.
❀ A vintage purse can become your "something old."
❀ Decorate with an extra-long ribbon for a bow, for minimal expenditure but maximum impact.
❀ Try a reversible bag for daytime-to-evening contrast.
❀ Be ecochic and have a go at making your own.

The two bags on the opposite page came from charity shops and were simply embellished with lace and ribbons in minutes.

Wedding planner tip:
If you are having a wedding dress made, ask the seamstress for a little extra fabric to make your own matching bag.

Wedding-day bag

This neat bag is the perfect accessory to have with you on the big day. It also works well for bridesmaids. This method is great if you come across a garment you love but that has marks that make it unwearable—and you don't need a sewing machine. I used both the lacy outer fabric and lining of a top I discovered in a thrift store.

YOU WILL NEED:

A piece of rough paper, 8½ x 11 inches

An old top or blouse in a pretty fabric—
    preferably lined

A piece of plainer fabric if the top is not lined

3¼ feet of ¾-inch-wide ribbon

5 feet of narrower ribbon in the
    same color

Short length of even narrower ribbon

Cotton thread in matching colors

Needle, scissors, and pins

An embellishment, such as a button or brooch

METHOD:

1. Place the paper on the garment, with the short side aligned with the bottom edge of the fabric, so any pattern runs in the right direction. Pin in place and cut around it, then repeat with the lining fabric.

2. Fold the outer piece in half, with the right side of the fabric inward and short edges together at the top. Seam neatly down each side, about 2 inches in.

3. Repeat the above two steps for the lining, but leave a gap on one side of about 2¾ inches at the top.

4. On the outer layer, with the right side still inward, open up the bag and pinch out the bottom two corners. Stitch horizontally across each corner to form equal triangles (see opposite page). Repeat the above step for the lining material. Turn through the outer layer so the right side now faces outward.

5. Take a piece of ¾-inch-wide ribbon and pin all the way around the neck of the outer layer, until the ends just touch. Cut the ribbon to this length and unpin. Hem the ends of the ribbon by ¼ inch.

6. Pin the ribbon back onto the outside of the bag, about 2 inches from the top, making sure that the gap in the ribbon is centered. Sew on with two rows of stitching, close to each edge, to make a casing.

7. Now, the tricky bit: Place the lining bag inside the outer bag so the good sides are facing each other. Stitch together at the top edge all the way around, about ½ inch in.

8. Pull the lining bag up, and pull all of the fabric through the hole in the lining. Sew up the hole, push the lining back down into the outer bag, and shake into place.

9. Sew a small, wrist-sized loop of ribbon to the lining, 2 inches down from the edge, on the opposite inner side to the gap in the ribbon casing.

10. Cover the loop ends with a vintage button, small corsage, or brooch.

11. Thread the thinner ribbon through the ribbon casing and gather as a drawstring. Tie in a bow and voilà!

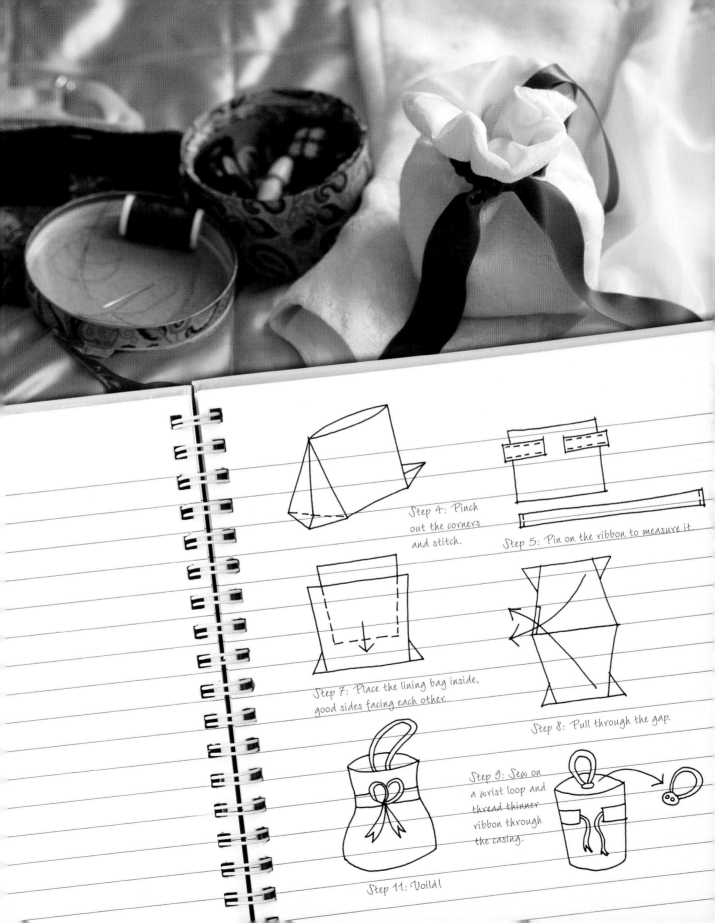

Step 4: Pinch out the corners and stitch.

Step 5: Pin on the ribbon to measure it.

Step 7: Place the lining bag inside, good sides facing each other.

Step 8: Pull through the gap.

Step 9: Sew on a wrist loop and thread thinner ribbon through the casing.

Step 11: Voilà!

* Alternative papers
From tree-free to recycled, handmade to petal pressed

* Wildflower-seed paper
An easy-to-master method to make your own gorgeous recycled paper

* Fashionable printing
Old-fashioned letterpress to modern waterless techniques

* Making your own
Ideas to get you started and where to learn craft and art skills

* E-weddings
Virtual invitations and wedding Web sites

* Greener registries
One-of-a-kind presents, charity registries, and rainforest-friendly guest books

The Invites

The invitations are the first hint guests will have of your wedding style. I find it helps to let your choice of venue inspire the design: intimate or formal, high glam or laid-back. Ecofriendly invites can be some of the most beautiful you'll find, as old-fashioned art and craft techniques become newly desirable. Letterpress printing, for example, can give you crisp formality, or you could choose a quirky design from an ecocard designer—or learn how to do it yourself.

Alternative papers

Choosing an environmentally friendly paper is a simple way to instantly turn your invites a shade greener. Handmade papers and creatively produced, recycled cards will make your wedding stationery distinctive, too.

Recycled paper
This is widely available in a range of colors and finishes. A 100 percent–recycled paper has a slightly rougher texture than virgin fiber, so for that "brand-new" paper sheen, opt for a blend of recycled content and virgin Forest Stewardship Council (FSC) paper. You can now find pure-white recycled paper, too, although you may want to choose an obviously recycled "fleck" finish as a design statement. The most eco-conscious option is postconsumer recycled, which has already had one use as a newspaper or magazine. See the Directory on page 208 for paper suppliers.

Forest Stewardship Council (FSC)
FSC-certified paper (www.fsc.org) is made from sustainably sourced timber. It is produced using virgin fiber so trees are felled, but new trees are replanted and protected rainforests are never destroyed. When talking to your printer, ask if the paper he or she is using is FSC accredited, and check for the logo.

Map paper
This is made by cutting old or out-of-date maps into sheets and envelopes. Each piece is unique. This is a great option for a couple who likes to travel.

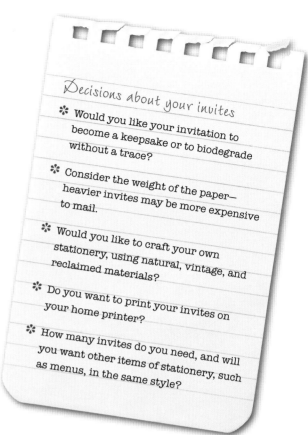

Decisions about your invites

❋ Would you like your invitation to become a keepsake or to biodegrade without a trace?

❋ Consider the weight of the paper— heavier invites may be more expensive to mail.

❋ Would you like to craft your own stationery, using natural, vintage, and reclaimed materials?

❋ Do you want to print your invites on your home printer?

❋ How many invites do you need, and will you want other items of stationery, such as menus, in the same style?

Tree-free papers
These are produced using other naturally occurring fibers, such as coffee and banana skins. They are available in either plain sheet form or as ready-made cards you decorate yourself. Some of the papers mentioned may be made in developing countries. As long as the paper is fair trade, this is a great way to ethically support a country; however, because of the transport distances, they will leave a larger carbon footprint than papers made locally.

Ellie Poo paper
Handmade from elephant dung, this paper carries no odor and is perfectly safe to use. Made using the fiber that passes naturally through the elephant from its wild diet (usually grasses), it is washed a number of times. The resulting paper is cream colored with an attractive natural flecking. Another alternative is Rhino Poo paper, while locally made Sheep Poo paper offers fewer "paper miles" in sheep-rearing nations.

Banana paper

This is made using the waste fibers from banana plantations. Mixed with postconsumer, recycled content, the resulting paper is naturally speckled and incredibly strong, with good environmental credentials. Try using it to make paper decorations and flowers (see page 162), as well as invitations.

Handmade paper

Handmade paper can be plain or include different natural materials, such as petals, grasses, seeds, and leaves. Try coordinating your paper with the table decorations, or even with your flowers. Pink rose petals are gorgeous in paper and can be scattered on wedding party tables to continue the theme.

Seed paper

Perfect for the natural wedding, seed paper can be planted by guests as a reminder of the day. It is available ready-made, or try making it yourself (see my method on the page 94).

Recycled and homemade envelopes

You can buy recycled envelopes, but to craft your own, take a square piece of paper that fits around your invite and draw faint pencil lines across the diagonals. Take any corner and fold across to half an inch past where the lines cross. Repeat with the opposite side, then fold and glue the bottom point in place. Fold over the top triangle to form a neat, square envelope.

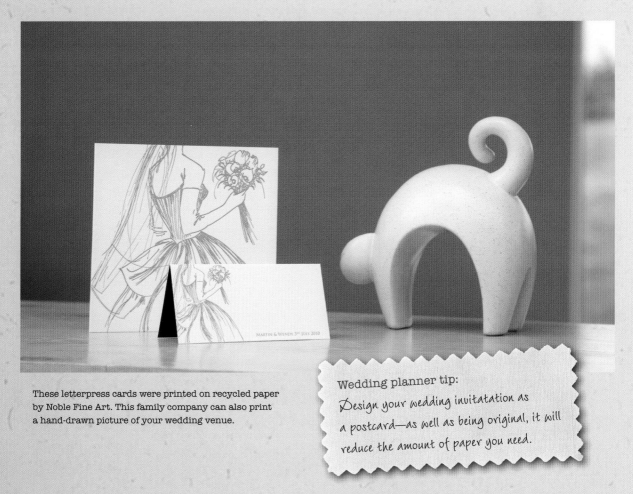

These letterpress cards were printed on recycled paper by Noble Fine Art. This family company can also print a hand-drawn picture of your wedding venue.

Wedding planner tip:
Design your wedding invitatation as a postcard—as well as being original, it will reduce the amount of paper you need.

Wildflower-seed paper

The measurements for this recipe depend on how much paper you would like to make. Try it out with a few sheets of scrap paper first, to get a feel for the technique. It can be messy, so you might want to work outside. I like to add wildflower seeds, but you could also use petals or foliage.

YOU WILL NEED:

At least 2 dry tea towels

A stash of scrap-paper offcuts

Deep bowl for blending

Electric hand mixer

Mesh tray (available at artists' supply stores)

Large, waterproof, flat container (larger than your mesh tray and at least 4 inches deep)

1 packet small wildflower seeds

1 damp tea towel

METHOD:

1. Lay your clean, dry tea towels to one side of your waterproof container.

2. Shred your scrap paper into small pieces and place them in a deep bowl. Cover with water.

3. Using your hand mixer, carefully pulse to purée the paper and water into a pulp.

4. Fill your large, waterproof container with water up to about 3½ inches, and stir in the paper pulp.

5. Scatter in the wildflower seeds, mixing thoroughly (alternatively, you can scatter the seeds over the damp paper in the tray, after step 7).

6. In one, quick movement, slide your mesh tray into the pulpy water and lift it up, so that you have a fine, even covering of pulp on the mesh. If it is too thick or uneven, plunge the tray back into the water.

7. Scrape the excess water from the underside of the mesh tray with your hand, and place the tray on a dry tea towel, mesh-side down.

8. Roll the damp tea towel into a smooth, flat wad, and use this to press carefully all over the new paper while it is still in the tray, to squeeze out excess water. Wring out the tea towel between presses.

9. Turn the tray upside down and pat gently to allow the paper to release onto the other dry tea towel. Make sure that the paper is as flat as possible before leaving it to dry.

10. Dry for at least twenty-four hours, then use it to make invites, place cards, favor boxes, and other stationery.

Wedding planner tip:
If you find your paper is sticking around the edges of the mesh tray when you flip it over, try using the underside of the tray instead.

You can use your paper to cut butterflies to hang from thin thread as decorations.

Follow this diagram to make favor boxes.

Simply fold small pieces in half for plantable place cards.

Tie on ribbons to make wishes tags.

These invites from Mandalay are printed on 100 percent-recycled paper, and the colorful ribbons are made from recycled plastic bottles.

Fashionable printing

Whether you prefer the smart, traditional look of letterpress or the rustic individuality of hand-carved wood blocks, there are plenty of printing styles to explore. Ecoprinting methods have developed rapidly, so you don't have to compromise on style or ethics.

Be bold with color and explore motifs that fit with your theme. A winter wedding I attended had a striking black-and-white color scheme, and the bride had designed the invitations to match, embellishing them with fine ribbon. The wedding was held at the elegant eighteenth-century Assembly Rooms in Bath, where Jane Austen would have danced, and the invite decoration was a chandelier in silhouette.

Vegetable-based inks

Inks made from natural vegetable oils are much kinder to the environment than regular petroleum-based inks. Many ecoprinters specialize in "veggie inks," and other printers now offer them as an alternative. The color choice and print quality are just as good as standard inks.

Waterless printing

Conventional printing emits thousands of tons of volatile organic compounds (VOCs) into the atmosphere every year and uses vast quantities of water. Waterless offset printing is a revolutionary method that uses no water in its process and has the added benefit of wasting less paper.

The print quality is thought to be better than conventional printing, with a full range of colors. A selection of printers offering this method is listed in the Directory.

Letterpress

This elegant, old-fashioned method of printing is enjoying a reviva and lends a touch of old-school glamour to an event. Many letterpress companies still use the original hand-operated antique machines, so their energy consumption is minimal. With an amazing range of typefaces, and the ability to print onto heavy paper stock, it is a fantastic choice for wedding stationery.

DIY

For smaller numbers of invites, using your household printer can be a thrifty option. Larger quantities may use many ink cartridges, which can be expensive, so it may be cheaper to have them printed professionally. Always recycle your empty cartridges—often charities will collect them or, alternatively, have them refilled to reuse.

Designer ecostationery

Many companies can both design and print your invites. If you would like to find an artisan craft printer, research local art colleges, check press and local Web sites for open studios, and try the crafters' Web sites such as www .etsy.com. Some will design a custom invite especially for your big day. Others offer an off-the-rack range of stationery that you can personalize with your own wording. Choose designers using recycled, handmade, or tree-free paper, embellished with natural and reclaimed materials.

Always ask for a written quotation listing the items and quantities, and overorder slightly, as you may make mistakes or have last-minute guests.

Wedding planner tip:
Order or make some blank place cards, in case you want to invite more guests just before the wedding.

Making your own

Hand-crafting your own invitations is fulfilling and can give stunning results. You could design and create a card from scratch or embellish a plain, ready-made ecocard. Collage and simple printing techniques are easy to master, and there are some quick-fix decoration tips below. Spend a lazy Sunday afternoon playing with ideas to see what works for you both.

Printing stamps and natural prints
This is perhaps the simplest way to craft cards. For a vintage-themed wedding you could invest in some antique wooden printing stamps, like those on page 97. Use letters of varying sizes and typefaces to create a simple but fashionable design.

You can find stamps online or at flea markets and antique fairs. Keep an eye out for unusual patterns, such as lovebirds or flowers.

One of my favorite ways to print natural designs is to use fresh leaves. Choose a leaf with a prominent vein pattern, brush ecopaint onto its back, and press it onto a card or paper. Use a single color with a variety of leaf shapes for a contemporary effect. For more ideas and methods, *Printing by Hand* by Lena Corwin has lots of lovely techniques, including stencilling.

Collage
Cutting, sticking, and layering materials can produce a wow-factor card, even if you are a relative craft novice. Plan your pattern first, and draw around a template for regular shapes. Use recycled and reused papers or magazine pages, vintage fabrics, and antique buttons.

Calligraphy
If you are having an intimate wedding, a beautifully handwritten invitation is a delightful indulgence. If you feel your own handwriting isn't up to the task, you could ask a friend or find a professional calligrapher.

Tips for home-crafted cards

❋ Design your invitations to minimize paper wastage.

❋ Consider how your embellishments will fare in the mail. If you are worried, mail a trial invite to yourself to check that it survives.

❋ If you don't have the skills to make the invites you would love, why not learn them? Workshops are available for techniques such as screen printing and letterpress.

❋ Bear in mind the number of cards you will be making, and keep to a process that you feel comfortable repeating.

❋ Find ecocraft supplies online (see the Directory on page 208 for details).

Linocuts

Linocutting involves carving a design into a small offcut of linoleum (supplies are available from art stores and aren't expensive). You can easily create letters and intricate designs and then print them onto your chosen paper. The block is re-inked between each print, so every card has a charming one-off quality. Check local art colleges for courses, or learn the skills and get expert advice at a craft studio (see the Directory on page 208). If you don't feel artistic, it's easy to trace an existing design onto the lino.

Woodcuts

Woodcutting is a more skilled method, where you carve the design into a block of wood with chisels. For this, you will definitely need to invest some time mastering the techniques, but the finished woodblock will make an amazing ornament and memento of your day.

These invites show three easy homemade styles. Use a hole punch, and tie with raffia or vintage or re-used ribbon, looping in vintage buttons or other decorations.

Screen printing

The ink is squeezed through a stencil onto the paper or card below. You can design and cut stencils yourself or buy them ready-made. It's possible to screen print onto a variety of media, from handmade paper to vintage textiles. For instructions and inspiration, see *Simple Screenprinting* by Annie Stromquist.

Wedding planner tip:
Try framing one of your invitations as a lasting reminder of your special day.

DIY invite inspirations

Decadent ribbons and fabrics, paper butterflies, and watercolor paints—they all add that extra wedding sparkle. Delight in selecting from the range of natural and vintage ornaments at your fingertips. Browse vintage origami books for inspiration—there are some beautiful folded patterns that you can use on cards. I also recommend *Nature Printing* by Laura Donnelly Bethmann; *Good Mail Day: A Primer for Making Eye-Popping Postal Art* by Jennie Hinchcliff and Carolee Gilligan Wheeler; and the stationery section at www .allthisismine.com.

Simple embellishments

Ribbons are a fantastic and quick way to give cards a professional finish.

* Tie together a paper insert and an outer card using a wide ribbon for elegant simplicity.
* Use three strands of thin ribbon in contrasting colors for a candy-stripe theme.
* Fashion sumptuous ribbon bows for a decadent look.
* Layer heavy vintage ribbon and delicate lace for perfect winter style.

Quick ways to add your personal touch

Find ready-made, tree-free cards and decorate them with natural and reclaimed materials.

* Salvage fine wire and shape it into simple shapes such as butterflies or flowers. Fix to the cards using small sewing stitches.
* Hand-color one or two elements of a black-and-white card with watercolor paint or colored inks.
* Print an insert for a bought card on your home printer; assemble the invite by tying it with natural raffia.
* Gather ribbons around a card and fix them in place by threading them through an antique button.
* Glue dried petals in a pretty pattern.

Vintage stationery

* Search out antique postcards or photo cards. Use them as they are (if not already written on) or mount them onto recycled card stock. Stamp with your chosen text, and embellish with white ribbon and buttons for an individual twist.
* Collage an invite using vintage magazines—fashion titles work especially well. Choose a stylish era such as the 1950s—perfect if you will be wearing a 1950s-style dress.
* Cut squares of reclaimed fabrics and mount them onto card stock, then decorate with paper butterflies and brightly colored ribbons for a summery look.
* Trace a 1960s fabric pattern to make your own linoleum stamp, and print this onto handmade paper for a touch of retro style.

Your raw materials

* Natural raffia
* Vintage buttons
* Dried flowers
* Lavender stems
* Vintage lace
* Salvaged wire
* Antique beads
* Velvet ribbon
* Shells (sustainably sourced)
* Hemp twine
* Organic cotton string

Wedding planner tip:
Tint the paper, fabric, and trimmings for your invites naturally with strong tea or beetroot juice.

We filled this fair-trade card holder with antique cards, mixed with handmade, vintage-style invites by Jessie Chorley.

Escort cards and wedding Web sites

Not all items on the usual list of additional stationery are necessary, and you may prefer to opt for invites only. Think about combining elements when possible, such as having the wine list on the menu, to keep your "paper footprint" smaller.

Escort cards

This American tradition has become popular worldwide and is a novel way to help people to find their seats. Guests' names are written on small cards (with the table number on the back or inside) and then showcased in a variety of ways, to fit your theme.

Fair-trade, wire card holders come in an array of shapes and sizes. A cream or white heart with scalloped name cards gives a romantic look. The card holder can be hung on a wall or placed in the garden and reused after the wedding. Suspend your escort cards from an antique birdcage for a striking display, or use rustic wooden vegetable crates or vintage mirrors to create a fabulous backdrop. For travel enthusiasts, tie named brown-paper luggage tags onto an antique leather suitcase.

Thank-you cards

Photo thank-yous are popular and can be prepared by your photographer, or you can print them at home on recycled cards. Alternatively:

❖ Send all the guests small packets of seeds, wrapped in personalized paper sleeves and tied with vintage ribbon.

❖ Be kitschy and send each guest a postcard from your honeymoon location, complete with a "Wish You Were Here" motif.

❖ Save cardboard food or drink boxes from the reception to craft into pop art–style cards.

❖ Keep the petals from your bouquet and use them in handmade paper thank-yous.

E-vites and paperless weddings

E-vites, or virtual invitations, are the greenest option, and if you are a whiz on a computer, you can create something delightful. Alternatively, there are nifty design companies that will design a fabulous e-vite for you, complete with a sumptuous, addressed e-envelope. Designs range from minimalist chic to lavish traditional, and you can send thank-yous by e-mail afterward.

Include a link to your wedding Web site for guests to RSVP and find event information, such as directions, accommodations, and the registry. With no paper costs or postage to pay, e-vites are a thrifty option. But remember to make a small batch of paper invitations for those guests without Internet access or who will treasure an invitation for years to come.

Wedding Web sites

These are still a fairly new phenomenon but are growing in popularity. You can give Web links to local places to stay; ask for guests' special needs, such as dietary requirements; and add fun, personalized information, such as photos of the bridal party. Think about including a song request page for the DJ or band and a link to your online wedding registry.

After the wedding, the site can be updated with highlights, photos, and thank-you messages, and you can ask guests to upload their own photos from the day. See the Directory for wedding Web site providers.

Wedding planner tip:
Build your own wedding Web site and have it hosted by a solar-powered Web host for a truly eco-online experience.

Greener registries

With more people marrying later in life and setting up house before the big day, there is less need for the traditional kettles and ironing boards. Wedding registries today can be for anything and everything, and they should reflect your values and style as a couple. If you want to include details on your Web site, remember that you will need to decide on the list beforehand.

Ecohoneymoon fund

Ask family and friends to contribute to your honeymoon fund, perhaps for two weeks in an ecolodge in Botswana or five days in a tepee at the Glastonbury music festival. There are some fabulously romantic honeymoon options close to home, from cool camping to ecochic boutique hotels; for more inspiration see page 192.

Ecofriendly guest books

Guest books capture the memories and sentiments of the day. Look for recycled, FSC-accredited or tree-free papers, and covers made from locally sourced, salvaged wood. Or try embellishing the cover of a plain book with your own design of pressed leaves, shell buttons, and fine wire. Guests could be asked to sign a special item, such as a photograph, or a piece of handmade paper that can be framed for posterity.

One idea I've seen work beautifully is for each guest to bring a leaf, then have the collection fused in glass to produce a lasting artwork.

A wedding list with a difference.

Ref no.

www.oxfamunwrapped.com

We're celebrating our big day with a gift list from Oxfam Unwrapped. It's packed full of gifts that will make a big difference to people worldwide. Simply visit the website, type in our reference number and choose from our selection. Thank you.

Ethical stores

Register with an online ecostore (see the Directory for suggestions). They stock an amazing array of brilliant, energy-saving gadgets, from solar panels to windup radios, as well as natural beauty and home wares. Most supply truly fair-trade products, so you can shop safe in the knowledge that your ethics are in good hands.

Other ecopresents

❖ Charity registries such as www.oxfamunwrapped.com offer fantastic selections of "gifts" that help countries around the world requiring aid.

❖ Set up a donation Web site, such as www.justgiving .com, to give to a charity close to your heart.

❖ For one-of-a kind gifts, ask your guests to make you something themselves, from jam to cushions, sculptures to renovated furniture.

❖ If you want truly one-of-a-kind presents, make a request for "anything secondhand," from retro children's board games to a French antique chest.

❖ Perhaps you've always dreamed of owning a patch of native woodland. A wedding fund means your favorite people can contribute to something that you will appreciate for years to come.

Wishes trees

These are charming. Plant a small tree or branching shrub—perhaps a blossoming fruit tree—into a decorative pot. Place it somewhere guests will have space to sit and write, and provide a stack of paper luggage tags or cards with ribbon or raffia ties.

Guests note down their message, tie it onto the tree, and make a wish. After the wedding, you can collect the tags into a book or special box for safekeeping.

* **Food for all seasons**
  Sourcing your food and choosing a caterer

* **Finding produce you can trust**
  Organic and biodynamic, plus foraging tips and edible flowers for the adventurous

* **DIY catering**
  Recipe ideas and growing your own fruit and vegetables

* **Lou's homemade chutney**
  Easy to make from windfall apples

* **Eating outdoors**
  Barbecues, picnics, and campfires

* **Drinks for your celebration**
  From local wines and organic cocktails to homemade lemonade

The Menu

Food to share with friends and family; a meal to celebrate the beginning of your marriage—that's the essence of a wedding reception. You can make it a formal occasion with the best organic, local, and seasonal caterers or try picnicking in summer fields, barbecuing on the beach, or hosting a fashionable tea party. Some of the most enjoyable meals are those to which guests each bring a dish, so everyone can join in.

Food for all seasons

Planning your menu around seasonal food is the most environmentally friendly choice, as the wedding meal is usually the element of the day with the largest carbon footprint. Often, fruit and vegetables are flown thousands of miles so that we can enjoy them out of season, and most people have lost track of whether products are locally made or grown, or imported.

Try to buy direct from local greengrocers, orchards, dairies, and farmers' markets, and ask where the produce comes from. Seasonal foods usually taste better, and they are cheaper, too. See our Seasonal Fruit and Vegetables calendar on page 216.

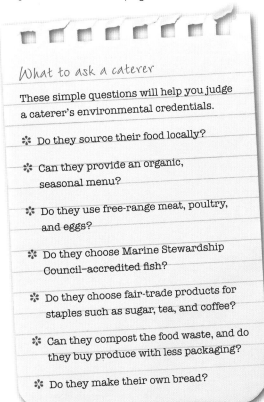

What to ask a caterer

These simple questions will help you judge a caterer's environmental credentials.

✳ Do they source their food locally?

✳ Can they provide an organic, seasonal menu?

✳ Do they use free-range meat, poultry, and eggs?

✳ Do they choose Marine Stewardship Council–accredited fish?

✳ Do they choose fair-trade products for staples such as sugar, tea, and coffee?

✳ Can they compost the food waste, and do they buy produce with less packaging?

✳ Do they make their own bread?

Farmers' markets and artisan producers

Farmers' markets are brilliant places to buy directly from local growers and suppliers, and everything from wonderfully flavored organic vegetables to handmade macaroons, local cream to free-range chicken is available. Make a beeline for small, artisan makers who take pride in the food they create. The bread on page 116 is from the United Kingdom's Thoughtful Bread Company (www.thethoughtfulbreadcompany.com), which uses traditional methods and foraged herbs. Find other artisan producers through our Directory.

Meat and poultry

While organic is the most sustainable farming method, all meat is considered to have a high environmental impact. To reduce your wedding's carbon footprint, why not choose recipes that combine a little free-range meat with a delicious variety of vegetables and other ingredients? This will also be more economical.

Catering choices

Your choice of menu will depend on your wedding style, together with your budget. If your venue is an ecohotel, then you will probably be tied to using its in-house caterers. But if not, specialist caterers can prepare the freshest organic meals, using ethical and local produce. Similarly, you can find dedicated vegan and vegetarian caterers. Look in the Directory for our favorites.

The most expensive option is a three-course, sit-down, plated meal, served at individual tables by a waitstaff. If you have a large guest list, or are on a budget, a buffet or tea party will be more manageable.

Finding produce you can trust

*C*hoosing ethical, organic, and sustainable produce is good for farm workers, the environment, and your health. Whether you are using a caterer or buying your own, free-range poultry, sustainable fish, fair-trade staples, and pesticide-free vegetables are all now widely available. For a real hands-on experience, try foraging wild foods.

Organic

Produce labeled as organic is grown without the use of synthetic pesticides, fertilizers, drugs, antibiotics, or wormers, and it is subject to strict regulation. Farmers are encouraged to control pests with natural predators and companion planting, and genetically modified crops are banned. Land that is used to grow food or rear animals must be "chemical free" for a minimum of two years before organic certification is awarded.

Biodynamic

This established method follows the astronomical calendar to determine when to harvest, plant, and cultivate crops. It is based on a self-sufficient farming system, producing natural animal feeds, manures, and fertilizers on-site. Herbs and special natural preparations (some of which contain animal products) are also used to achieve healthy, strong plants. Demeter (www.demeter.net) is the international certification body.

Fair trade

Many staple foods are grown in developing countries, where farmers rely on exporting cash crops to earn a living. Unfortunately, child labor, low wages, and dangerous working environments are all too common. The Fairtrade Foundation was set up to stop this. Look for the international FAIRTRADE certification mark.

Marine Stewardship Council

The MSC (www.msc.org) promotes sustainable fishing practices and protects the marine environment around the world, and its blue logo guarantees traceability back to a certified source. It helps to ensure that resources are not overfished and that destructive fishing methods are banned. The MSC can also tell you where to buy certified fish.

Edible flowers

Many varieties can be used in salads and as edible decorations. As with foraging (see opposite page), ensure that flowers are picked at their freshest, grown without the use of pesticides, washed thoroughly, and used quickly. Research your subject and get to know what is safe to eat. Nasturtiums, calendula, geraniums, elder, and rosemary flowers can all be used in recipes and make delectable garnishes.

Slow Food

The Slow Food movement, which began in Italy, is winning worldwide supporters as it says no to fast foods, plastic bags, unethical produce, pesticides, and food that has traveled thousands of miles. Instead, it promotes traditional and artisan foods that taste wonderful and that are produced sustainably and ethically, with pride and passion (see www.slowfood.com). Grow your own vegetables, bake bread at home, ask your grandma to write down her favorite recipes for you, and try regional products crafted from ingredients grown close to home. Slow your pace of life and enjoy food you have taken time to prepare for your wedding feast.

Foraging

Consumers are beginning to realize the foragers' feast available to them on country walks and in their gardens. Some ingredients, such as wild garlic, are easy to spot—just follow your nose. Mushrooms, on the other hand, take a practiced eye. Read a good foraging book before you start, to ensure that what you are picking is safe to eat, and never dig up plants. (My top tip is to avoid picking anything around the base of trees, which may have been popular with dogs.)

Wedding planner tip:
Check that caterers can provide sauces and condiments made with free-range and organic ingredients, too.

DIY catering

Preparing your own food is a wonderful way to put your personal stamp on the day and to keep your spending down. You can be sure of the origin of your ingredients and lavish lots of care and attention on each dish.

A meal for sharing

Do things a little differently with your catering, and ask family and friends to bring something delicious for all to share, perhaps suggesting either sweet or savory, to keep a balance. Noncooks can bring a bottle of something fizzy instead. If you feel uncomfortable asking, propose this as your wedding gift—much more useful than another toaster. Not only will guests enjoy a wonderful range of flavors, but those with special diets will be able to bring a dish that suits them.

Easy recipes for homemade menus
Wild-rice salad ❖ spiced, toasted seeds and nuts ❖ potato salad with baby onions ❖ honey-roasted ham ❖ poached fish ❖ homegrown leaf salads brimming with radishes and tomatoes ❖ spinach and wild garlic ❖ char-grilled peppers and mushrooms ❖ homemade rolls with tasty herb spreads ❖ free-range mayonnaise

For winter
Root-vegetable stews ❖ spicy curries ❖ tasty soups ❖ hot flatbreads ❖ bowls of ratatouille

Follow with simple desserts
Huge pavlovas filled with organic whipped cream and homegrown berries ❖ homemade ice creams or sorbets.

Big platters

Vintage platters are easy to find in thrift stores and markets. Seat guests at long trestle tables, and place your large platters of different dishes down the middle.

Growing your own

If you have a garden or yard, then it's possible to grow some of your own organic produce for your wedding. There is nothing more satisfying than seeing vegetables spring up from a packet of seeds, or fruit from an unpromising twig in the ground. You can buy organic seeds and plants at nurseries or online. Remember to choose sustainable, peat-free, organic compost so that natural peat bogs are not depleted.

You will need to plan ahead and allow sufficient time to grow the ingredients that you would love to have on your menu. Some, such as broccoli, need many months to mature, while salad leaves can be raised from seeds in a couple of weeks. Soft fruit, such as strawberries, raspberries, and blueberries, take little effort and are ideal for summer weddings; serve them in meringues or on your cake (see page 124) or use them to make jam.

Windowsill herbs

Herbs such as oregano, coriander, and sage are easy to grow, and even if you don't have a garden, you can keep them in small pots on your kitchen windowsill. Raise them organically, and they will instantly add another dimension to your wedding salads. You could also try fiery chili plants.

Wedding planner tip:
Serving bowls, platters, and large dishes can all be rented if you don't have enough.

My friend Justyn made
gorgeous tarts and salads for
this garden-party wedding.

Lou's homemade chutney

Jams and chutneys are some of the most rewarding things you can make with garden or foraged produce. Windfall apples, homegrown onions, damsons, and plums can all be easily cooked down and served in small pots with your meal. This is my favorite chutney recipe, which works every time.

MAKES ABOUT 12 SMALL POTS

INGREDIENTS:

1½ pounds windfall apples of any type

4½ pounds red tomatoes

½ pound red onions

½ pound white onions

1 pound unrefined sugar

2½ cups organic cider vinegar

½ pound golden raisins

1/2 teaspoon dried chili flakes

1 teaspoon ground cumin

1 teaspoon ground ginger

A good pinch of sea salt

A good pinch of ground black pepper

You will also need a deep-bottomed saucepan or a preserving pan.

METHOD:

1. Peel and chop the onions, tomatoes, and apples, and place in a deep pan over medium heat.

2. Carefully pour in the cider vinegar and stir gently. Add the sugar and raisins, and stir.

3. Mix in the chili flakes, cumin, ginger, salt, and pepper.

4. Simmer for about 2 hours, until the apples are tender and the pan contents have been reduced by about a third. During cooking, skim the surface with a wooden spoon to get rid of impurities from the unrefined sugar.

5. Wash your jars and lids in hot, soapy water, and place them on a clean baking tray, mouth side up.

6. Put the tray in a preheated oven at 350°F for 10 minutes to sterilize. Then remove and cover with a clean tea towel until you are ready to use them.

7. Fill the jars with the chutney and immediately screw on the lids tightly.

8. Allow to cool before labeling the jars with the contents and date. This chutney can be used straightaway, but for a more mellow flavor, leave it for a couple of months before eating.

Wedding planner tip:
Peeling the tomatoes first gives a better, more luxurious texture—loosen the skins by parboiling them before peeling.

As favors, with ribbon ties and luggage tags with guests' names.

You can present your chutney in different ways, depending on your wedding style.

Served simply in small mason jars.

With a fabric lid cover and natural raffia bow.

Eating outdoors and perfect tea parties

Checkered blankets and pitchers of homemade lemonade, picturesque sunsets, and fields full of swaying daisies—picnics make a glorious setting for a wedding reception. They are inexpensive and fun to organize, too. Look for good-quality, vintage wicker picnic baskets in charity shops and markets—they are full of retro charm and incredibly useful. I found the basket pictured above in my local charity shop, in perfect condition, for only a few pounds. I customized it by adding vintage crockery and homemade napkins. Baskets often will come complete with place settings for eight.

Ask friends and family to bring along plates of sandwiches or boxes of salads and homemade fries. And don't forget the bottle opener and glasses.

For big gatherings, rather than transporting large quantities of heavy crockery, you might want to pack some ecofriendly Tupperware. From plates made out of waste palm leaves (from ethical, sustainable plantations), glasses made from corn starch, and cellophane sandwich bags to wooden cutlery—it is easy to source biodegradable options. See the Directory for suppliers.

Barbecues and campfires

Barbecues are fantastic for beach weddings, or why not set one up in your garden for an informal celebration? Look for local, sustainable, and fair-trade charcoal; it's now much easier to find. Check with the beach that barbecues are allowed.

A small campfire—on a beach, in woodlands, or by a river—is the perfect accompaniment to an outdoor wedding. Use it to make hot drinks as well as meals. Baked potatoes can be cooked in the embers but need to be checked regularly, and baked apples with sugar and raisins make a mouthwatering autumn dessert.

Above: Hand-rolled jasmine tea. Right: Rocks East—perfect for woodland receptions.

Pig roast

Mobile pig roasts are available from farmers or caterers and are always set up outdoors. A whole pig, preferably organic, is roasted on a traditional spit, and served with bread and salad. It can feed a large number of hungry people with ease.

Transporting food

Plan ahead how you will take food to an outdoor location. Old, wooden vegetable crates lined with clean tea towels can be used to pack plates and boxes of food; cover with another tea towel to protect from insects. When emptied, the crates can be turned over and used as small tables.

Tea party

Serve dainty sandwiches, homemade scones with jam and clotted cream, tiny cakes, and pots of hot tea. In the summer, offer iced tea or fruit cordial instead. You can make heart-shaped scones with a special pastry cutter and serve savory cheese scones as an alternative. Try individual cakes decorated with pale pink icing and shimmering sugared flowers (see page 135), and handmade fondant fancies in pinks and greens.

Specialty teas

Tea has become fashionable, with all kinds of single varieties, including connoisseur hand-rolled teas. Or choose blends of black, green, and white tea, or herbal teas. Caffeine-free rooibos (redbush) is rich and mellow. Always go for organic and fair trade, and for zero tea miles, make infusions from the garden.

❊ Spring: fragrant jasmine, delicate Darjeeling, white peony tea with rose petals, foraged young nettle

❊ Summer: cooling peppermint, citrus-scented green teas, elderflower, or refreshing fruit infusions

❊ Autumn: traditional Earl Grey, warming ginger, vanilla rooibos, or soothing chamomile

❊ Winter: smoky Lapsang souchong, rich Assam, frothy chai latte, or spiced cinnamon apple

Drinks for your celebration

Wines produced by exciting local vineyards will keep down your wine miles; go to a tasting at the vineyard or a nearby supplier so you can try before you buy. The wines on the opposite page come from the award-winning Avonleigh organic vineyard in north Somerset, England, and Wickham Vineyards in Hampshire, England.

High-quality organic wines and champagne-style sparkling wines are now widely available, and biodynamic vineyards produce some of the world's finest bottles. Check labels for low or zero sulphur content if you have dietary sensitivities.

Organic fruit wines have a long history but are generally not drunk as often as grape wines. Choose from varieties such as elderberry, plum, ginger, or tayberry. See the Directory on page 211 for suppliers.

Artisan cider and perry

Specialist ciders and perry (pear cider) are becoming popular alternatives to wine. There are some delicious, light, champagne-method varieties that rival sparkling wines in taste; I particularly like Ashridge from Devon. Serve in tall, elegant, stemmed glasses. If you have an orchard and cider press nearby, you could even have a go at making your own cider.

Mulled wine and mulled cider

Rich with the taste of cinnamon, orange, and spices, these mixes bring a glow to a winter wedding and are simple to prepare at home. Try adding a glug or two of brandy before serving for extra warmth.

Homemade cordials and lemonade

Fragrant elderflower cordial and zesty lemonade are superb nonalcoholic alternatives that are easy and cost-effective to make yourself. Buy organic, unwaxed lemons and scrub thoroughly before use. Pick your elderflowers from traffic-free spots, and wash thoroughly. Use fair-trade, unrefined sugar and store in recycled bottles. In the winter, offer guests your own mulled elderberry cordial made from dried elderberries and spices—delicious and great to keep colds at bay.

Mineral water

Ideally, serve tap water in pretty glass jugs to reduce water miles and waste. If you do opt for bottled, choose a nearby supplier who sources from a local spring and buy in large containers. Recycle bottles and see if you can buy on sale or return.

Organic cocktails

Bramley & Gage produces delicious liqueurs from homegrown soft fruit using traditional French methods. For an elegant, summery drink, mix sparkling wine or water with raspberry liqueur and serve with a raspberry in the bottom of the glass. Delicious.

HEDGEROW SLING

¼ cup organic sloe gin

2 tablespoons fresh lemon juice

2½ teaspoons Bramley & Gage blackberry liqueur

Soda water, or naturally sparkling water

Shake the sloe gin and lemon juice with ice and strain over fresh ice into a Collins glass. Top with soda water and float the blackberry liqueur. Garnish with fresh blackberries.

The Cake

The wedding cake has to be the most delicious
element of the day. You can really have fun with it,
regardless of how formal the wedding. There are all
kinds of exciting possibilities, from brightly colored
cupcakes to classic elegance or a modern sculpture in
chocolate. Some of the prettiest cakes I've seen have
been iced plainly, then decorated with soft-petaled
roses, or had each tier topped with close-packed
raspberries. The only limit is your imagination.

Choosing your perfect cake

Everyone loves a wedding cake, and you can find styles to suit the most unusual of celebrations. Some cakes sit happily as part of an afternoon tea at a relaxed summer garden party, while others can take center stage in the grandest country house. You can be greener with your cake by choosing local, seasonal, and ethically sourced ingredients and save pennies by having the cake double as your favors or dessert.

Your cake personality

Your choices of venue, dress, and flowers can help you find your cake "personality." Look for inspiration in your wedding-day notebook (see page 32) and books such as *Cakes for Romantic Occasions* by May Clee-Cadman, which is lovely, and *Cake Chic* by Peggy Porschen. The www.thecaketress.ca Web site has some amazing designs, too. Save offcuts of dress fabrics and ribbon to help when selecting decorations.

At one outdoor wedding, with playful ribbons in the trees and the groom arriving in a decorated camper van, the bride chose a birdcage cake by the Utterly Sexy Café (www.utterlysexycafe.co.uk), iced in pastel blue with ornamental garlands of magenta icing flowers. But if your own dream wedding is more formal and Grace Kelly in style, with a floor-length gown and hundreds of guests, an elegant and traditional white, tiered cake, with fresh white roses, is gorgeous.

Colors and decorations

Cakes can be created in any color imaginable, from bright turquoise to shocking pink. You could even have each tier be a different color. With combinations of icing, ribbons, and flowers, it is easy to match your cake to your wedding color scheme.

For a dramatic look, team a base of black icing with delicate, white, filigree-piped icing (see page 125). This is easy to do at home yet gives a professional result.

If you are not keen on icing, simply stack light sponge cakes. Add a generous dusting of icing sugar and decorate with plump, seasonal berries.

Baking your own cake can be an enjoyable challenge and help your budget, too. You may be surprised at what you or your family can achieve. Alternatives, such as tarts and mousse cakes, can be served as part of a meal.

Remember that your cake needs to feed all of your guests, so calculate quantities carefully. Bear in mind the time of year you are getting married, as the availability of seasonal ingredients will vary.

Professional cake bakers

An online search or asking locally will turn up a host of cake bakers. Prices and ethics vary, so shop around and always check references. Book a tasting session before you order, to try different types of cake and icing, and don't be afraid to ask it they use organic and local ingredients. To reduce your food miles, try to choose a baker who is closer to the venue; some venues will even bake the cake on-site.

If you would like to do the decorating yourself, many bakers will provide a plain iced cake: This keeps costs down, and you can exercise your artistic flair. Alternatively, you can have a homemade cake professionally iced and decorated—ideal if you love your mom's fruit cake but don't want her to worry about her icing skills.

Your ingredients

Maybe you can barter with neighbors for fresh eggs or make your own fruit preserves. Local magazines and Web guides will lead you to nearby farms, mills, and farmers' markets. See the Directory for Web sites listing producers in your area. By taking the time to choose your ingredients carefully, you will rest easy knowing your cake does not have a large carbon footprint or contain synthetic additives—and it will taste great.

Rachel at Planet Cake (www.planet-cake.com) uses eggs from her own hens. She crafted the flowers from sugar paste, so it's all edible.

Wedding planner tip:
Cover plain cake boards with a layer of white icing to give your display a professional finish.

Baking your own cake

Making your own wedding cake needn't be daunting. It means you know exactly what it contains, and you can choose your own favorite recipe. Plan ahead and have a trial run if possible, especially for the decorations. Take photographs of the finished cake, make an equipment and ingredients list, and time the whole procedure. By estimating how long it will take to decorate your final cake, you can calculate when it needs to be baked.

Fruitcake can be kept in an airtight container for weeks but sponge cake only has a shelf life of a few days. If you are planning on keeping a top tier for a christening, always choose fruitcake, as it will freeze easily. For recipes, *Delia's Complete Cookery Course* is my must-have bible. You can make your own decorations (see page 132) or buy them ready-made; with either it's possible to create beautiful designs with minimal effort. The Planet Cake

(www.planet-cake.com) buttercream stack on page 120 shows how simple you can go. Dip strawberries in slightly cooled, melted dark chocolate; leave them to set on wax paper; then zigzag them with melted white chocolate using a piping bag.

Mom's finest

Family members and close friends will be thrilled to be involved and might even make the cake their wedding gift to you. Have a discussion beforehand and show them photos and sketches so that they understand the cake you are envisioning. Renting the baking tins or stands and buying ingredients will help them out. Remember transportation on the day of the wedding: Check if they are happy to deliver the cake to the venue, and provide sturdy boxes or an extra pair of hands if required.

Tiered cakes

This formal design usually has three or more tiers of different sizes, suspended above one another on pillars. Always ask for white plaster or timber pillars and timber dowels to keep things natural. Unless you are experienced with tiered cakes, my advice is to leave this style to the professionals. An easy way to create an elegant tiered effect, without the worry, is to use a tiered cake stand. You can rent one of these and then simply place a cake, on its board, on each level.

Stacked

This is a more modern style—most of the tiered cakes shown in this chapter are stacked. Here, the tiers are placed directly one upon the other. When kept simple,

this can be a beautiful option, and it can be decorated with elegant trimmings, such as ribbons and vintage jewelry. You still need dowels and boards, but the home cook can easily achieve a two-tier, stacked cake.

Contemporary designs

Many bakers now offer extraordinary contemporary cake designs, from striking sculpted chocolate to edible rice-paper creations. Whether you dream of a breathtaking, long and low, ice-white winter scene or a tall tower of dark chocolate curls, the only limit is your budget.

If baking your own, search in specialist shops for unusual cake-tin shapes, and see page 135 for instructions on making chocolate curls.

Maya made her own wedding cake. Here she is showing filigree icing, using her own design. The dots make it an easy technique to master.

Versatile cupcakes

These colorful cakes have become extremely popular. They can be served as a cake course or pudding, or even used as favors. Recipes range from traditional sponge cakes to minifruitcakes, gluten free to spiced carrot. All can be baked and decorated by the most inexperienced of home cooks, and there will be a flavor to suit each of your guests, regardless of taste or dietary preference. For display ideas, see page 136.

Vintage

Decorate the edge of the paper liners with lace and ribbons, neatly secured with a small dot of icing. Serve on floral vintage crockery with miniature, antique cake forks.

Traditional

Use pure-white icing and select only white decorations, such as small sugar flowers or delicate dots of filigree icing. Try icing and decorating the cakes in three different styles and then mixing them up. White cupcakes on a tiered cake stand can give the impression of a traditional, tiered cake.

Delicious cupcake tips

- Use muffin tins and muffin liners, and fill only halfway. This means you will have room for piped icing.
- Why not gather your bridesmaids and friends for an evening of baking/ Make sure to bake a few extras to "test"!
- Pipe butter icing onto the tops—a star-shaped nozzle is best. Ice from the edge of the paper liners inward.
- Alternatively, "flat ice" the cakes with a small palette knife dipped in hot water.
- You could also pipe on whipped cream and decorate with fresh seasonal fruit—but prepare these cakes at the last minute, and be sure to refrigerate them.

Contemporary

Choose bright shades of icing, or even glossy dark chocolate, and combine with fresh flowers in vibrant shades for a dramatic effect. Try placing a fresh flower between each cupcake on a tiered cupcake stand. Arrange the blooms just before serving so that they don't wilt, and check that they are safe to be in contact with food.

Natural

Match vanilla icing with unbleached paper liners and sugared petals made from edible garden flowers that are in season (see page 135). Decorate the stand with raffia for a naturally beautiful display.

Top: Elegant white from www.countrycupcakes.com.
Above: Sugar flowers are easy to find and quick to apply.

Lou's gluten-free lemon cupcakes

You can find all sorts of options for regular sponge cakes — the classic formula is to weigh three eggs and use the same amount of flour, butter, and sugar. Below, I've given you my favorite gluten-free recipe, as these can be more difficult to track down. This recipe can also be baked in one large tin.

MAKES 12

INGREDIENTS:

Paper muffin liners

1½ stick of unsalted butter

¾ cup superfine sugar

2 beaten eggs

½ cup ground almonds

Finely grated zest and juice of 1 unwaxed lemon

¼ cup gluten-free plain flour

½ teaspoon gluten-free baking powder

5 tablespoons polenta flour

METHOD:

1. Preheat your oven to 350°F.

2. Line a muffin tin with grease-proof muffin liners in a color of your choice (remember, they are going to be on display).

3. Beat the butter and sugar together until pale and creamy, then stir in the eggs and almonds, and then the lemon zest and juice.

4. Sift the gluten-free flour and baking powder into this mixture; add the polenta flour, and stir gently until combined.

5. Carefully spoon the mixture into the muffin liners, being careful not to spill any on the sides. Only fill them halfway (to allow room for the icing).

6. Bake for 20 minutes or until the cupcakes are firm to the touch. If in doubt, gently test with a skewer: if it comes out clean, they are done. (The cakes will have risen but will still be below the tops of the muffin liners.)

7. Transfer to a wire rack and allow to cool completely.

Use a star-shaped piping nozzle — it's quick and easy.

Group on a vintage cake stand for a tea party.

Show them off in individual sundae dishes.

Create a traditional cake effect by stacking on a tiered cake stand.

Alternative cakes

Of course, you don't have to serve cake at all—your wedding is an opportunity to be original. Many of these alternatives can be made by home cooks, although some do require skill. If you would like your tiered wedding cake to double as dessert, choose a sponge recipe and serve with homemade fruit coulis or local ice cream.

The cheese "cake"

Wheels of your favorite local cheeses can be stacked as you would a traditional cake and decorated with fresh flowers or fruits—ideal if you don't have a sweet tooth. Cut in the usual way, and serve to your guests after the meal with homemade crackers and seasonal fruit. (Bear in mind that blue and soft cheeses can have a distinctive scent and are not recommended for pregnant women.)

Fruit tartlets

Tiny mouthfuls of buttery pastry, delicious patisserie cream, and fresh fruit are delightful and easily made at home. Fruit tartlets can be displayed as you would cupcakes (see page 136); include a slightly larger tart for the bride and groom to cut and share.

Minimeringues

These are light and sculptural—and a perfect, thrifty choice. Topped with fresh cream and berries or sugared edible flowers, they can also be your dessert.

Little mousse cakes

These perfectly formed stacks of vanilla sponge, whipped cream, and fresh fruit or chocolate mousse can be assembled with a small, removable patisserie ring (found in cookware shops and online). Dust with powdered sugar and top with chocolate leaves or marzipan fruits for a light and delicious cake substitute, and serve with tea on dainty china. Vary the mousse flavorings to give different colors, such as strawberry pink or blueberry lilac.

Sweet individual cheesecakes

These can look completely at home at a wedding if they are carefully baked and decorated. Mixing dark and white chocolate in your fillings gives a contemporary, marbled effect. If serving as a pudding, add a fruit coulis to cut through the richness and to add a touch of elegance.

Mini wedding cakes

These are literally miniature versions of a full-size cake, with perfectly smooth icing and sumptuous decorations (see page 137). They look elegant stacked on a tall stand and are ideal as favors—but you're best off asking a local cake specialist to make them for you.

A note about chocolate

Cocoa beans come to us from countries with a favorable growing climate, such as Venezuela, so they will always have a larger carbon footprint than local produce. But there are plenty of organic and ethical brands; ideally, check for fair-trade accreditation marks.

If you are feeling adventurous, you could try making your own raw chocolate—it's surprisingly easy. You'll find courses, instructions, and cocoa beans to order online (see www.chocolatealchemy.com or www.williescacao.com). The results are delicious, and you can make them sugar free, too. Plain, raw chocolate is also stocked in health-food shops.

Decorations for your wedding style

From velvety roses to delicate gypsophila, fresh flowers and foliage will give your cake a seasonal, natural charm. There are also many inventive vintage and homemade possibilities. Nonedible decorations will need to be removed before the cake is sliced, so let your caterer know that you want to save them as a memento.

Flowers and fruit

Make the most of seasonal blooms. The cake on the opposite page has been dressed with flowers that can easily be found in the late spring: early roses, and white lilac and bluebells from a friend's garden. If you are on a budget, you could choose a small posy for your bouquet and transfer it to the top of the cake after the ceremony. Some flowers, such as nasturtiums, are edible, but make sure that any flowers you use have been grown without pesticides.

Colorful fruit can turn a plain cake into a culinary masterpiece. Heap seasonal, ripe berries onto each tier of a stacked cake and dust with powdered sugar for a mouthwatering, professional display.

Raffia

One of the natural products I like best, raffia can be used to great effect on cakes of all types. For simple country chic, take about twenty long strands and tie them in a big bow around the waist of a white, iced cake.

Vintage jewelry

If you are wearing vintage jewelry with your wedding outfit, you could incorporate a matching brooch into the design of your cake. Marcasite and anything sparkly works well, particularly antique dress clips and buckles. Tie a long satin ribbon around the top tier of your cake and fix your find to the center of the bow for instant glamour.

Ribbons and trims

Search online shops and visit vintage fairs for all manner of trimmings, from ribbons and tassels to Christmas bells. A large, blousy antique silk flower looks fabulous on the top tier of a cake, teamed with vintage ribbons in a matching color. Or make your own sugar-paste ribbons and bows, as seen on the cake pictured on the left (see page 134 for how to do it).

Tea lights

These are stunning for a late-evening wedding. Place the tea lights in small, clear glass holders; site them on the top tier of a royal, iced cake; and surround with small, fresh flowers. Be sure to choose unscented, plant-wax candles, and check that other decorations are not flammable.

Paper flowers

If you love trying new crafts, try making beautiful paper flowers for your cake (see the paper-flower bouquet on page 163). There are courses and many books on the subject that include patterns. You could even fold origami flowers from edible rice paper.

A beginner's guide to icing types

Royal icing
Traditional, hard sugar icing, usually bright white.
Fairly easy to make and use if you have a steady
hand and the right equipment, but it sets like rock.
Royal icing can only be used with fruitcakes, which
must be covered with marzipan first.

Sugar paste (regal ice)
A soft, roll-out icing. Popular and easier to use than
royal icing, it gives a rounded edge to the cake
tiers. You can decorate the cake by crimping:
making small, decorative pinches with a tool
found in sugar-craft supply shops.

Pastillage
Absolutely beautiful. An advanced technique
in which sugar dough is formed into intricate
sculptures. I would advise you to take a course if
you want to learn the skills.

Butter icing
Delicious and easy to whip up. Usually used for
small cakes or large sponge cakes, it can give
a sharp edge to the tiers. The UK version is ivory
colored and has a short shelf life due to the
butter content. US buttercream often uses white
vegetable shortening for a purer white icing.

Recognize this cake? It's the same basic,
butter-iced stack shown on page 120. Rachel
from Planet Cake has made a space with two cake
boards for florist Tallulah Rose to fill with flowers.

Sugar paste, glitter, and chocolate curls

Edible decorations are ideal for a natural wedding—at the end of the big day, whatever is not eaten will biodegrade. It is easy to make your own, but if you are not sure of your sugar-crafting skills, you can also buy ready-made sugar flowers and decorations.

Edible cake toppers
Sugar-paste figurines of the happy couple are available ready-made in a range of styles to match your theme, or you could have a go at making your own. You can also buy sugar flowers of many kinds (the roses on this page came from a local shop).

Glitter you can eat
Edible glitter is a relatively new concept in cake decorating but is proving popular as a dusting for cupcakes and to give a sparkle when added to the icing of larger cakes. You can find glitter made from natural gum arabic as well as from sugar.

How to make sugar-paste bows
A simple yet extremely elegant way to decorate a plain cake with the minimum of fuss. Tint some sugar-paste icing to match your wedding accent color and roll out to about ¼ inch thick.

Cut long, straight ribbon strips of matching width (1 inch works well) and secure them around the bottom of your cake tiers with a little sieved apricot jam. Make a bow using the same width strips and allow it to dry and harden before fixing it to the cake. Cut the ends of the bow into little Vs for a professional finish. These work particularly well on square, tiered cakes.

Edible decoration ideas

❊ Giant chocolate buttons—choose organic fair-trade chocolate in white, milk, or dark

❊ Seasonal fresh fruit

❊ Chocolate shapes and leaves—make your own or buy from online stores that promote fair trade

❊ Sugared edible flowers

❊ Rice-paper flowers—easy to make (or buy) and highly decorative

❊ Sugar-paste ribbons and bows

❊ Edible glitter

Make your own chocolate curls

YOU WILL NEED:

Fair-trade organic chocolate (dark should be
   70 percent cocoa solids)
A cold, hard surface, such as a granite countertop
   or a chilled baking sheet
A sharp knife and flexible palette knife
Wax paper for the finished curls

METHOD:

1. Melt the chocolate slowly in a double boiler (or in
   a bowl over a pan of just-simmering water), stirring
   gently with a wooden spoon.
2. Take off the heat and spread the chocolate onto
   the cold surface in a thin layer using the palette
   knife. Allow to cool.
3. Once cooled and solid—but not rock hard—use
   a sharp knife or cheese shaver to scrape up into
   individual curls. Place on wax paper to set in a cool
   place or in the fridge for a couple of hours.

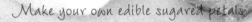

Make your own edible sugared petals

YOU WILL NEED:

Wax paper
Superfine sugar
1 egg white and a few drops of water
Three handfuls of fresh, edible flower petals,
   washed and patted dry
Small artist's paintbrush

Wedding planner tip:
For a professional touch, marble the
chocolate for decorations such as leaves or
curls by partially mixing white and dark.

METHOD:

1. Put a sheet of wax paper on a baking tray and dust
   with sugar.
2. Lightly whisk the egg white and water in a bowl until
   just frothing, then paint the mixture onto the petals
   in a thin layer. Hold the bottom tip of the petal
   carefully in your fingers or with a pair of tweezers.
   Be careful to cover the whole petal surface with
   egg white, or your flowers will brown.
3. Dust the petals with sugar, and place them on the
   wax paper. Repeat, then allow to dry completely
   in a warm, dry place. They keep for a few days in a
   dry, airtight container but will go soggy in the fridge.

Showing off your cake

A wedding cake can make a wonderful centerpiece for your celebration. Elaborate icing deserves to be fully appreciated, so try placing your cake in front of a vintage mirror to allow your guests to see all angles. For a relaxed outdoor reception, you can achieve a more rustic look by setting your cake on a tree stump or upturned antique vegetable crate. Make sure that it is level and out of the way of inquisitive children and pets.

If you are having a small wedding with one long trestle table of friends and relatives, position the cake in the middle as a focal point, and surround it with flowers, foliage, and candles. This works particularly well for winter and Christmas-themed weddings, and it means the cake will be center stage in photos.

Imaginative touches

Flowers, foliage, clean driftwood and shells, leaves, petals, and fruit will all create beautiful and unusual displays around the base of your cake. Save magazine pictures and look at www.devondriftwooddesigns.com for inspiration. Ivy cascading down the length of a table makes for a magical effect.

Any individual cake, whether it's a cupcake, tartlet, minimeringue, or pastry, can be presented as a favor for a guest. If the cake is delicate, or you are worried about flying insects, place it in a clear cellophane bag tied with a ribbon or raffia. Cellophane is made from plant cellulose and is fully biodegradable.

For unusual and theatrical table settings, serve cupcakes in vintage teacups, or group perfect minicakes on vintage shelves or in an apothecary's chest.

I always enjoy hunting around flea markets and antique centers, and collecting Victorian tiered wire and wrought-iron plant stands. These work beautifully as alternative cake stands. Clean thoroughly and revive with a coat or two of natural paint; afterward, you can reuse the stand for your plants.

Displaying cupcakes

* Show them on vintage, glass cake stands or plates gathered from thrift stores or flea markets—keep an eye out for rare colored glass. Group the stands together in threes for a stylish effect.

* Rent a professional, tiered cupcake stand. These are available in anything from three tiers to eight. You can decorate the edge of each level with a thin ribbon in a complementary color.

* Use a Wilton stand. This is a professional wire stand that holds each individual cupcake at a slight angle, like branches on a tree. It is a good option if you are only having a small number of cakes, but make sure the stand you order is for the correct number.

* Be bold and line your cakes up along a narrow table. Interweave them with flowers, petals, leaves, ivy, and raffia.

* Place a small flag or sail in each cake with the name of the guest. Alternatively, have the names iced directly onto the cakes as edible place "cards."

* Serve in pretty 1950s glass sundae dishes as a thrifty dessert.

* Add interest with gorgeous cupcake wrappers. Available in recycled paper in pretty and intricate designs, such as butterflies, you wrap them around the plain liners to add a professional finish. Try making your own from real petal paper for a thrifty cake upgrade; find templates and instructions online. You can scallop the edges with craft scissors.

Rachel made several variations of these Planet Cake blossom minicakes, and we displayed them in a set of vintage champagne saucers.

Wedding planner tip:
Square wedding cakes are much easier to cut and serve neatly than circular cakes, and they look elegant, too.

* **Seasonal blooms**
  Local and organic flowers, working with a florist, and DIY workshops

* **Growing and sourcing flowers**
  From delicate wildflowers to elegant lilies

* **The perfect bouquet**
  Styles for all dress shapes, and how to tie your own gorgeous bouquet

* **Individual displays**
  Unusual and inventive ways to "dress" your wedding with flowers

* **Herbs, pots, and foliage**
  Delicious table herbs and decorative ideas for foliage

* **Petal confetti and giving flowers away**
  What could be more natural than petals? Presenting your confetti with style.

The Flowers

Local and seasonal flowers, and cottage garden and prairie blooms, are in vogue—and not just at green weddings. The beauty of seasonal flowers is that the variety and color palette change throughout the year. I love the seasonality of flowers, and choosing a species associated with a particular time—early spring anemones or midsummer poppies—means that the bloom will always remind you of your wedding date.

Seasonal blooms

Seasonal flowers are the best choice for a natural wedding, especially when grown locally. There are gorgeous natural options in every season (take a look at the Seasonal Flowers calendar on page 217 for inspiration). The hellebores used as hair decorations on page 183 bloom from late winter, while evergreen foliage and fruits can be used to make stunning displays.

Themes throughout the year
* ❊ Spring: early flowering bulb plants in unusual pots, such as brightly colored hyacinths
* ❊ Summer: vintage vases filled with roses, peonies, and sweet peas
* ❊ Autumn: big bunches of golden sunflowers or late-season rich colors and seed heads
* ❊ Winter: festive wreaths with rosehips, crab apples, fir cones, and cinnamon sticks, or hand-crafted paper flowers (see page 163)

Most store-bought cut flowers travel hundreds, if not thousands, of miles by air or sea, creating an enormous carbon footprint. Instead, buy local flowers from farmers' markets and smaller, cottage-garden growers. Seasonal blooms are less expensive and often fresher, too.

Organic, fair-trade, and biodynamic flowers
Look for flowers certified by organizations such as the Soil Association or USDA, or grown biodynamically under the Demeter mark, which have not been sprayed with pesticides. If you have your heart set on a flower that isn't in season at the time of your wedding, try buying fair-trade blooms. There are many other ethical and ecocertification systems worldwide, so check for their marks (see pages 110 and 217 for more information).

Floral workshops
Why not create your own wedding flowers? Once you know the basics, you can easily make arrangements, boutonnieres, and posies. Floristry workshops are a great place to find out tricks of the trade, the equipment required, and which flowers complement one another. My friend and talented florist Rachel, from Tallulah Rose Flower School in Bath, England, taught me how to make the hand-tied bouquet shown on pages 146–147.

Jane Packer's *Flower Course* is an excellent book full of hints and tips, and among Paula Pryke's titles, I particularly recommend *Wreaths and Bouquets*.

Planning with a florist
You may wish to employ a professional florist, especially for a large celebration. Good florists are worth their weight in gold and can create breathtaking arrangements to suit your wedding style and budget. Choose one who can provide you with seasonal flowers, preferably from a local source, and follow-up references. Flowers can be one of the most expensive wedding services, so ensure that you have a budget in mind before you meet. And take along a picture of your wedding gown and proposed hairstyle to help determine the design of your bouquet.

Wedding flowers
* ❊ Bridal bouquet
* ❊ Bridesmaids' bouquets and men's boutonnieres
* ❊ Flower-girl posy or willow wand
* ❊ Church arrangements
* ❊ Pew ends or chair decorations
* ❊ Table centerpieces and mantelpiece displays

Jo Illsley of Bath Organic
Blooms grew the flowers
for her own wedding.

Growing and sourcing flowers

Even if you are a novice gardener, it is relatively easy to grow your own flowers to cut and arrange in vases, or to raise plants and herbs to display in their pots. You can glean ideas from open gardens and plant nurseries and borrow books such as Sarah Raven's *The Cutting Garden*. If you are planning your wedding a year in advance, see what is in bloom in the month you are marrying. Friends may have established plants already in their gardens or be happy to plant some for you. Join an organic gardening organization to get advice and referrals.

If you are lucky enough to have a yard or a good-sized kitchen garden, set aside one bed for your wedding flowers in the weeks leading up to the big day. Saving seeds or joining a local seed swap, where you swap spare seeds with like-minded people, are thrifty options.

Wildflowers

Although it is tempting, never pick wildflowers while out on country walks. Take photographs instead. Wildflowers, such as cow parsley, are an enormous benefit to local wildlife and support natural ecosystems. If you would like to display wildflowers at your celebration, grow your own at home for harvesting before the big day. Seeds are available from garden centers or online sources such as www.organiccatalog.com and can be grown with little effort. Or, buy them from cottage-garden growers.

Wildflowers are extremely delicate and can wilt shortly after cutting, so grow them in unusual pots and containers and, instead, display the flowers as growing plants.

Farmers' markets

These are wonderful places to buy local flowers directly from the growers. Imagine galvanized buckets full of wide-open anemones or bunches of vibrant cornflowers tied with raffia. Take a camera and ask questions about the flowers' origins and longevity. Many growers will be able to take orders for collection the day before the wedding. When buying local, seasonal flowers, bear in mind that weather conditions may affect what is available.

Cottage-garden flowers

In colors from pure white through to sugar pinks and pale lilacs, on to deep purples, I love fragrant sweetpeas. Try using a single color for an elegant but informal bridal bouquet. Cut the stems quite short, and tie them with wide, satin ribbons for a professional finish.

Dried flowers and wheat sheaves

Naturally dried wheat sheaves, barley sheaves, poppy heads, and teasels can be bunched together, as you would a hand-tied bouquet, and secured with raffia or ribbon as a centerpiece. For a more elaborate display, mix in fresh blooms such as roses or lavender. A mini version makes a lovely, country-style bridal posy.

Wedding planner tip:
Calla lilies are easy to grow at home and make a striking bridal bouquet, suitable for the most glamorous of weddings.

Your bouquet style

The shape and color of your bridal bouquet or posy will be guided by your dress. Have you chosen a formal gown, which will be best complemented by an elegant bouquet filled with structured flowers and foliage? Usually, these bouquets feature a single color theme. Or, will you be wearing a cocktail, prom-style, or flowing empire-line dress, which will be enhanced by a gentle, delicate posy? For these styles, you could try wildflowers or cottage garden blooms in a mix of colors, loosely tied together.

Bouquets for dress styles

* Formal: hand-tied bouquets
* Prom style: spherical posies or pomanders
* Empire: single flower

More petite brides benefit from teardrop-shaped bouquets to lengthen their frame, while taller brides can carry off spherical arrangements with ease.

Don't forget that bouquets, like dresses, can be embellished to match your theme. You could include vintage lace (which has been used to wrap the sweet william bouquet to the left), antique brooches, or an heirloom silk flower.

Bridesmaids

Usually bridesmaids will carry a smaller version of the bridal bouquet. As an alternative, think about pomanders, corsages, or posies, and keep to the same color scheme but vary your choice of flowers.

Flower girls

Small posies or pomanders, or even decorated willow wands, make perfect floral accessories for children. Make sure that they are reasonably robust, as they will inevitably be thrown around with exuberance on the day.

Boutonnieres for the seasonal groom

Boutonnieres can add a special touch to a groom's outfit. Traditionally, boutonnieres are worn on the left, and the groom has a more elaborate design than his best man, ushers, and groomsmen.

Herbs make fabulous boutonnieres, whether teamed with a flower head or on their own. Rosemary signifies remembrance, so if there are family or friends who cannot be there, this is a nice way to remember them. Avoid using large, open blooms as these can

become damaged over the course of the day; compact, smaller flowers, such as roses, are classically elegant.

Fail-safe fixing

Florists often supply boutonnieres and corsages with magnetic fixings. In my experience, these are often not robust enough and do not work on more flimsy fabrics. Instead, ask for large-headed pins, which you can weave through the fabric and over the stem. If in doubt about how to do this, ask your florist to fix the boutonnieres and corsages on the morning of the wedding, or show the best man so that he can take on the task.

Wedding planner tip:
Fragrant, white-belled stems of lilies of the valley make an elegant yet fresh bouquet for all dress styles.

Bouquet tips

❋ To help wild- or cottage-garden flowers last, plunge the bottoms of the freshly cut stems into boiling or hot water, then put them straight into a vase.

❋ Take bouquets out of water half an hour before needed and pat the stems dry on a clean tea towel to avoid drips and water stains.

❋ Cover unsightly stems with wide, satin ribbons for an elegant finish.

❋ If arranging your own bouquet, remember to remove thorns or anything that could catch on your dress.

❋ Remove lily stamens, which can stain fabrics and skin.

Hand-tied wedding bouquet

This easy technique was taught to me by Rachel at Tallulah Rose Flower School. You can use whatever flowers are in season, in your preferred color scheme, and match the ribbon to a flower or your dress.

YOU WILL NEED:

Your selection of flowers

Foliage stems that complement them

Twine

Florist's shears or other tough scissors or pruning shears

3½ feet of ¾-inch-wide ribbon or vintage lace

A pin

3½ feet of 1-inch-wide ribbon or vintage lace

Fabric scissors

METHOD:

1. Condition your flowers by removing lower leaves, thorns, and stamens (which can stain clothing).

2. Separate your flowers and foliage into types, and lay each bunch in a group on your table.

3. Take the first flower—the largest type—and cross a second bloom over the top of the first in your hand (as shown above, in the second photograph from the left).

4. Select a different flower and cross it over the other two stems.

5. Turn the bouquet and add another flower or piece of foliage. Repeat until you have used each type of flower. Remember to keep turning your bouquet in the same direction, and to check the shape from every angle. Look in a mirror to help you judge if you are forming the flowers into a pleasing arrangement.

6. Continue turning and crossing stems until you have a tight, rounded bunch with a "twisted" stem shape.

7. Tie the stems securely with twine, then trim the ends with the shears so that they are all the same length.

8. Wind the narrower ribbon neatly around the stems so that at least 1 inch is covered. Secure with a pin.

9. Wrap the wider ribbon around the stems and tie it into a bow at the front, making sure the pinhead is covered. Trim the ends into pretty Vs with the fabric scissors.

10. Keep your bouquet in water until needed, but be careful not to submerge the ribbon.

Wedding planner tip:
I have used a number of different flower and foliage shapes, but kept it coordinated here by choosing only whites and greens.

Step 4: Add a third flower, crossing the stems.

Step 5: As you cross more stems, they make a "twisting" pattern.

Step 7: Cut all the stems to the same length.

Your finished bouquet.

Individual displays

Any container can be a potential vase. Vintage bottles, antique vegetable crates, goldfish bowls, rustic galvanized buckets, glass sundae dishes, enamel jugs, glass test tubes (with a single bloom in each), or wire mannequins—all will add personality to your displays. Most types of flower containers can be rented from your florist, or buy your own at flea markets, thrift stores, and online.

Vintage cut-glass and ceramic vases

These are wonderful for brightly colored, blousy, country-style blooms. Old varieties of roses, gypsophila, peonies, and tulips look fabulous simply bunched into vintage vases. Ideal for a garden-party wedding: Team with single flower heads displayed in vintage teacups and teapots brimming with flowers.

Contemporary

For a simple and effective display, float flower heads and delicate plant-wax candles in bowls of water. Thrifty yet stylish, this technique also works well for small ponds (use a fishing net to retrieve the candles).

Alternatively, hang single flower blooms on fine cotton thread at differing heights from beams, window frames, tree branches, or a string "line." Choose robust flowers, such as roses, and leave half an inch of the stem to tie the cotton onto. This can be stunning in buildings with delicate structures, such as orangeries.

For another elegant, modern look, line up mismatched old glass bottles and place a single bloom in each.

Hay bales

If you are using hay or straw bales for informal outdoor seating, try sinking a sturdy vase or bucket into the bale so that the lip of the container is flush with its top. Fill the vase half full with water and arrange your flowers. Place vases at the corners of the bale for maximum impact.

Wellington boots

Clean Wellington boots filled with flowers make a humorous and charming display. Although waterproof, the boots can be unstable when filled with water. To steady them, first fill the bottoms with heavy stones. Choose cottage-garden colors, arrange the flowers in a loose style, and set the Wellies on your tables. If you love this idea but are not keen on having boots on your tables, stand them in doorways and in corners to catch guests' eyes.

Jam jars

For an outdoor wedding, a wonderful way to denote an "aisle" is to hang recycled jam jars, filled with flowers, on wooden stakes or poles. To create a hook for the jar, tie floristry or recycled wire around the neck and twist it into a hook or handle. Short-stemmed sweet peas, cornflowers, and peonies look amazing displayed in this way. For a fairy-woodland theme, use minijars and single blooms hung on willow branches.

Herbs, pots, and foliage

One of the most ecofriendly ways to incorporate flowers into your celebration is by using potted plants and herbs. This allows them to go on living after the wedding and leaves no waste. At the end of the day, give your decorations to guests as lasting keepsakes.

Herbs as flowers and to eat

Herbs are some of my favorite wedding flowers, as they are so incredibly versatile. Sweet-scented herbs, such as lavender and rosemary, make gorgeous displays, while others, such as thyme and basil, can be eaten as part of the meal: Encourage guests to pick off the fresh leaves to accompany their food. (A zingy, home-grown tomato tart is enhanced by a few tender basil leaves, while rock hyssop is delicious on risottos.)

For table centers, you could plant herbs in antique terra-cotta pots tied with vintage ribbons, or choose herbs that come in natural coir pots. Decorate these biodegradable containers with natural raffia for a fully plantable decoration. You can also buy your own natural coir pots online from ecogarden suppliers: Choose minipots for small herb varieties or large ones for centerpieces. Try unusual containers, too, such as food tins with the labels removed, or vintage teapots.

Branches and blossoms

All year round, you will find interesting foliage in the garden, both evergreen and deciduous. If you are marrying in the spring, take advantage of the abundant blossoms on trees and bushes, from bright yellow forsythia to pale pink cherry.

Bare winter twigs and branches pruned from garden trees can be decorated with lanterns or with fresh flowers hung in minijars, for a fashionable room display. Boughs of catkins, soft leaf buds, or tiny blossoms look fabulous in tall enamel jugs or old milk churns.

Unusual pot plantings

From brightly colored daisies to tall, waving sunflowers, mini rose bushes to deep purple hyacinths, you can present growing flowers in interesting pots and containers.

❄ Group pots of small plants in odd numbers on tables. For a modern feel, use pots of the same size lined up in rows; for a country look, use different sizes grouped more loosely.

❄ For an outdoor wedding, plant small flower varieties in vintage wooden seed trays. Place these on the centers of the tables, and decorate them with matching ribbons.

❄ Use vintage ceramic vases as pots, and plant with wildflowers to bloom in time for your wedding.

❄ Daffodils, hyacinths, and snowdrops make an uplifting springtime display. Plant them into unusual containers, such as vintage tins and wooden bowls.

Evergreen ivy

Whatever the time of year, ivy can be found scrambling up walls and covering the ground, and it is easy to cultivate at home. Team it with large blooms, such as roses, for an elegant look, or with wildflowers for a more rustic feel. One couple on a tight budget was holding their reception on a barge. I draped the cabin with muslin and ivy bunches, transforming it from a plain, utilitarian interior into a mini wedding marquee.

Wind ivy around staircases and along tea light–dotted mantelpieces for a winter theme, or use it as the base for a wreath with pine cones and cinnamon sticks. (Check beforehand that you are not allergic to ivy.)

Petal confetti and giving flowers away

Biodegradable confetti is the only choice for a natural wedding. Don't be tempted to ask the guests to throw rice after the ceremony. Wild birds tend to eat it, and then it swells in their stomachs. Instead, choose natural petal confetti, either fresh or dried. It can be found in every color imaginable, to match any wedding theme. Some dried petal confetti will stain if it becomes wet, so if you are worried about rain, choose white petals to avoid accidents.

Dried petal confetti

As dried petals are much lighter than fresh, they take longer to fall through the air, giving more opportunity to catch that confetti photograph. The beautiful confetti on the opposite page came from British company Shropshire Petals. Here is a guide to the different colors available:

* Pinks: roses, peonies, hydrangeas, heather
* Blues: hydrangeas, delphiniums
* Yellows: sunflowers, roses, jasmine
* Oranges: marigolds, roses
* Whites: delphiniums, roses, hydrangeas
* Lilacs: hydrangeas, lavender
* Reds: roses, hydrangeas
* Greens: roses, hydrangeas

Fresh petals

The best flowers for fresh confetti are roses of any type—even the small, tight ones—as they have lots of petals. About twelve roses should be enough for a large basketful. You could ask local flower stalls for blooms past their best at the end of the day, which would otherwise be disposed of. Florists can also provide fresh petal confetti, as they may have flowers that are not good enough quality for displays, but are fine for use as confetti.

How to make fresh confetti
* Take two bunches of garden, local, or fair-trade roses.
* Wrap your hand around the whole flower head.
* Pull gently, in a twisting motion.
* The petals should come off in one bunch, leaving behind the center part of the bloom.
* Gently separate the petals into a bowl, basket, or paper cones.

Displaying and distributing your confetti

To minimize paper wastage, place your petals in one big glass bowl or basket, and ask guests to help themselves. Or give your flower girl a pretty basket of confetti that she can hand out to guests as they leave the ceremony. For an outdoor wedding, she could scatter petals down the "aisle."

Alternatively, you could make your own confetti cones out of recycled or handmade petal paper and arrange them in a basket, box, or bowl. A nice touch is to make the cones from seed paper containing the seeds of your confetti flowers (see page 94). Guests can then take home the cones and plant their own confetti.

After the big day

You may have decided to give all of your flower displays to guests, but if not, you could ask one of your bridesmaids to take them to a local retirement home. Displays will often last for a good week after the wedding. Floral arrangements made for churches and chapels may be left at the venue for other congregations to enjoy; check that the church is happy for you to do this. Table confetti, cake flowers, and displays that have been out of water for some time should be composted, but remember to keep any trimmings, such as ribbons, for reuse.

* *Natural decorations*
  From fruits and driftwood to pebbles, plus seasonal style tips

* *Original and unusual*
  Sky lanterns, ribbons, and bicycles

* *Vintage themes*
  How to theme your wedding with crockery, antiques, and fabrics

* *Handmade and DIY*
  From gorgeous paper flowers to natural soaps

* *Teacup candles*
  Find out how to make ecochic lighting

* *Decorations on a shoestring*
  Plus ethical buys and thrifty raw materials

* *A feast of homemade favors*
  Delicious truffles and scented lavender bags

The Decorations

Choosing a seasonal or vintage theme will make your decorations eye-catching without costing a fortune. Search out the best green suppliers and products hand-crafted by artisans, or try making your own. Decorating your wedding, whether a simple ceremony or a lavish celebration, with flair, will wow your guests and give your day its own unique atmosphere. And it is simpler than you might think to achieve a beautiful, natural wedding setting.

Natural decorations

Fruits, flowers, and foliage can all be used to style a wedding day (for more about flower displays, see page 148). Collect and beachcomb driftwood, pebbles, leaves, and twigs. By using objects from nature, sourced locally, you can be sure that your trimmings will have a minimal carbon footprint and will biodegrade or that they can be returned to their environment.

Ways with fruits, flowers, and foliage

❉ Fruit: Use as place holders by tying miniature luggage tags onto the stems. Guests can eat the fruit as part of the meal.

❉ Driftwood: Place clean, pale driftwood down the center of a long table and intersperse it with plant-wax tea lights.

❉ Leaves: Scatter russet or golden dried leaves on the tables, or wrap fresh leaves around candles.

❉ Blossoms: Gather blossoms and scatter them on tables and in gardens.

❉ Pebbles: Use as place holders by either painting on the name of the guest or tying on a small tag with rustic twine.

Beach weddings

Let your imagination fly with what is naturally available. Build sand castles with intricately molded buckets and jewel them with collected shells; they could outline an "aisle" or standing area. Draw patterns in the sand, gather pebbles to make heart shapes, and tie reclaimed fabric onto willow twigs to make gently swaying flags or wind catchers. Group together flowers and beachcombed driftwood in tin cans.

Seasonal ideas

❉ Spring: dainty wildflowers, spring bulbs, and pots of grasses and herbs. Choose from sweet-scented jasmine; exotic-looking hellebores; magnificent magnolia blossoms; and fresh, green foliage.

❉ Summer: bunting in the trees, antique galvanized watering cans bursting with local flowers, and potted strawberry plants from which guests may help themselves.

❉ Autumn: rich, red leaves and glossy berries; deep-colored blooms and willow twigs; teasels and other dried seed heads; pumpkins; decorative squashes; and rosy apples.

❉ Winter: plant-wax candles; log fires; storm lanterns; holly; winter-white flowers; natural ivy; fir cones; cinnamon sticks; and rich, sumptuous ribbons.

Trees and herb favors

Tiny trees in plantable coir pots make fabulous favors that will last a lifetime. Choose a native species, or try raising your own baby saplings from acorns and collected seeds. Baby herb plants are wonderful gifts, too; grow them in small, antique terra-cotta pots or present the plants in burlap bags. To make the bag, cut a square of natural burlap four times the width of the root ball, pop the herb roots into the center, and gather up the corners. Tie a piece of string, ribbon, or twine around the neck and fasten in a bow. See *Jekka's Complete Herb Book* and www.jekkasherbfarm.com for varieties and advice.

Homegrown
snowdrops in coir
pots are teamed with
Jessie Chorley's
handmade
table numbers.

5

Wedding planner tip:
Recycle Christmas decorations for a festive
theme—place delicate glass baubles in tall,
clear vases for a striking centerpiece.

Original and unusual

Stage a wonderful display with antique planters, old jam jars, and even bicycles—see if salvaged and recycled bits and pieces can be given new leases on life. We created the wedding notice on the left with two flea market–bought French wire plant holders and a handmade wooden sign, painted with natural paints.

For the garden-party wedding that you see throughout the book, I covered wooden trestle tables with plain white tablecloths, then laid beautiful vintage and secondhand lace cloths over the top. Cut-glass vases and jugs, collected over the years, were filled with country-style flowers, from blousy pink peonies to fragrant white stocks. In between these, I arranged old glass and silver candlesticks holding plant-wax candles.

The places were set with mismatched vintage crockery, and the look was completed by my homemade napkins, in different fabrics, tied with offcuts of ribbon. The result is something you could create yourself—add your own original elements and personality.

Sky lanterns

Drifting skyward on a summer evening, sky lanterns are a magical, romantic decoration. Made from paper, with a beeswax disk that you light to send them into the air, they are silent and completely biodegradable. They are much more environmentally friendly than fireworks, which will scare wildlife. Visit www.skylanterns.com, who delivers worldwide.

Ribbons in trees

For a seaside wedding, I decorated the branches of the surrounding trees with vintage and recycled ribbons and pretty glass lanterns. It worked for both daytime and evening. So quick and easy to put up, ribbons are a cost-effective decoration and look fabulous if cut long so that they can catch the breeze. Choose colors to complement your theme.

Bicycles

If your style of dress allows it, arrive at your wedding on a bike, with veil flying, for an amazing photo opportunity. Embellish your cycle to make it the perfect wedding transportation.

❖ Baskets: Fill the front basket with armfuls of seasonal blooms.

❖ Panniers: Secure the bridal bouquet onto the rear pannier.

❖ Signs: Direct guests to the reception with your bike. Hang a sign from the crossbar and decorate it with flowers and foliage.

Handmade wooden signs

If you need signs for your event, why not make your own from timber? Salvage wood—preferably planks with the bark still on the edges—and use a soldering iron to "write" onto the surface for a rustic effect. You could also use large printing stamps with waterproof inks or paints.

Mirrors

Prop antique or vintage mirrors from thrift stores and online auctions behind displays of flowers to create an illusion of depth. Or lay them flat and arrange pillar candles on top to reflect the light and, more practically, catch any wax drips. You can always change the color of the frames by repainting them.

Wedding planner tip:
Place jam-jar lanterns next to marquee tent pegs to help guests avoid tripping over the ropes at night.

Vintage themes

From 1970s flower power to 1950s chic to delicate Victoriana—vintage elements can fit both traditional and alternative weddings. If you are not sure where to start, find a vintage object that you adore, such as a teacup or candlestick, and build your decoration style around it.

Crockery

I love vintage—especially crockery. Everything from tea sets to cake stands, glassware to milk jugs. I started collecting years ago and now have a huge chest filled with my finds, which I rent to couples for their wedding or party (you can see a few of these pieces pictured on the opposite page and on page 171).

For your own, look in junk shops, at trunk sales, and in thrift stores to deck out your wedding at minimal cost. Don't forget that you can always sell crockery afterward. Once friends and family know that you are collecting for your big day, you will probably be showered with their collections to borrow or keep. Mix and match designs for a deliciously eclectic look, and place vintage teacup candles (see page 164) on shelves and tables, and in gardens. See the Directory for vintage rental companies.

Ornaments

Antique and vintage ornaments can all be used to great effect on tables and mantelpieces, and outdoors. Glass candlesticks, pretty ceramic birds, candelabras, and strings of beads are an easy way to theme your day. Pick them up at charity shops and flea markets for a small outlay, and donate them back to charity afterward.

Jewel favors

For female guests, buy small vintage brooches and pin them onto their napkins. This can be inexpensive, and it will create both a lasting favor and a fabulous decoration.

Bunting for all occasions

Bunting is ideal for weddings, silently dancing in the breeze, tied onto trees or around marquees. Debbie Coutts (www.tatteredandtorn.co.uk) made the gorgeous bunting on page 154. She uses only reclaimed and vintage fabrics and trimmings, tints them with tea and plant dyes, and sews the flags by hand. Try making your own, perhaps in different shapes, such as hearts or stars, and embellish it, with vintage buttons and ribbons.

Retro details

* 1950s teacups in single colors
* 1960s brightly colored art-glass vases
* 1970s floral tablecloths
* Victorian glass candlesticks
* Antique lace
* Vintage teacup candles (see page 164)
* Salvaged vintage newspapers
* Retro magazines

Delightful place cards

❋ Try vintage playing cards, traditional postcards, or antique photo cards. Write the names by hand in large letters in a contrasting color.

❋ Salvage retro magazines and cut out quirky ads or pictures to paste onto recycled cards.

❋ Secure vintage newspapers (sepia tones work well) onto recycled paper as a backing for a hand-printed name.

Handmade and DIY

*E*mbellish your wedding with delightful decorations skillfully handmade by local artisans, or make your own with natural, recycled, and biodegradable materials.

Paper and fabric flowers

Gorgeous and available in a rainbow of colors, these can be arranged in the same way as fresh flowers. Look for handmade paper blooms or choose fabric blossoms sewn with vintage materials; a bouquet fashioned from salvaged lace and silks can be just as beautiful as a fresh posy—and it will last a lifetime.

The paper roses on the opposite page were created by skilled maker Wendy Morray-Jones, who bases her designs on a vintage pattern book and cuts each petal individually. Search on the craft site www.etsy.com for techniques and inspiration.

Recycled sculptures

Artists and designers can craft unusual decorations out of reclaimed wire, wood, and metal, from tiny birds to delicate snowflakes. Group them together as a centerpiece or set them individually at each place setting.

Glass hanging ornaments

These catch the light beautifully and are usually handmade from recycled glass. Tie them onto willow branches or hang them from trees for an outdoor celebration.

Wooden name tags

These are great for decorations and also guest favors. Buy tags with a small hole in one end so that you can thread them with a ribbon, and tie them onto napkins or favors. Or else, make your own tags by salvaging offcuts of reclaimed wood and printing words or names onto them with old printing blocks.

Seating plans

If you are opting for a traditional, large, written seating plan, try displaying it on a timber easel, decorated with seasonal blooms and foliage, for a secret garden feel. Enclose it in a gilt picture frame so that you won't need to mount it onto card stock. Outside a marquee, use a blackboard on an easel for guests to write messages or to chalk up the menu.

For a striking display, suspend place cards from an antique birdcage. Alternatively, old rustic wooden vegetable crates or pretty vintage mirrors create a fabulous backdrop. Travel enthusiasts will appreciate named brown-paper luggage tags hung inside an antique leather suitcase, and for an outdoor wedding, simply tie them onto tree branches with natural raffia.

Soaps

Natural soaps make fantastic decorations and favors. Either buy them from a local, natural skin-care company or try making your own—look for soap-making workshops online or at the craft spaces in the Directory on page 208. Choose small soaps decorated with dried rosebuds or lavender, wrap in brown wrapping paper, and tie with ribbons and twine. Add a recycled paper name tag, and place on napkins for a gift and place card in one.

Wedding planner tip:
If you are making your own soaps, bear in mind that they will take about six weeks to "cure" and be safe to use.

Paper roses by Wendy
(www.wendymakesroses.com)
formed into a bouquet by
Rachel of Tallulah Rose Flower School.

Teacup candles

These are simple to make yet incredibly beautiful. Find your plant waxes and natural wicks from reputable suppliers to ensure that they are clean burning and ecofriendly, and buy teacups from thrift stores. After the wedding, clean the cups and either make more candles or use them for tea.

YOU WILL NEED:

Tiny rubber bands

Wooden cocktail sticks

A selection of pretty teacups and saucers

Natural wax, such as soy or rapeseed

Double-boiler pan or a heat-proof bowl and saucepan
    it can sit in

Natural wicks with metal sustainers attached

Wooden spoon

Scissors

METHOD:

1. Hold two cocktail sticks together and secure each end with rubber bands. Repeat until you have the same number of these as cups.

2. Heat the teacups by placing them in a warm oven for 5 minutes.

3. Melt a spoonful of wax in the double boiler or in the heat-proof bowl over simmering water. Gently dab onto the bottom of the metal wick sustainers.

4. Quickly center the sustainers in the bottoms of the cups. (If you prefer, you can use glue dots instead of wax.)

5. Place the cocktail-stick "wick holders" across each cup, threading the wicks between the sticks until they are secure and upright.

6. Pour the wax into the double boiler and heat until it melts and reaches the temperature recommended on the packet. Stir at all times and be careful not to overheat.

7. Carefully pour the melted wax into each teacup, making sure that the wick holders do not move. Fill to ½ inch below the tops of the cups.

8. Leave until completely set—do not move or shake the cups during this time.

9. Trim the wicks to ¼ inch long with sharp scissors.

10. Arrange at your wedding and enjoy.

Wedding planner tip:
Try mixing a little beeswax into your wax blend to give the candles a wonderful honey scent.

Step 5: Thread the wick up between the sticks of the "wick holder."

Step 7: Pour the melted wax to ½ inch from the top of the teacup.

Step 9: Once fully set, trim the wick to ¼ inch in length.

Decorations on a shoestring

For those on a tight budget, simply beg, borrow, and make everything you need. Freecycle is a great resource for finding items for free. After the wedding, recycle them back into the system or give them to charity (www.freecycle.org). Or, why not borrow eye-catching decorations from friends and family?

My money-saving tips include using timber picnic tables so that you don't need tablecloths and making your own bunting from pretty, secondhand bedsheets. Cut the sheets into rough triangles of the same size, and stitch them onto "ribbon" from the same fabric. Candy stripes or florals give different looks, or else, mix them up. Don't worry about frayed edges—they are part of the charm. Arranging your own flowers is also good for the budget: Garden varieties, such as hydrangeas, in simple, contemporary glass can look stunning. And for the ultimate fuss-free reception, host a picnic or barbecue—either of which needs little adornment other than the bride and groom, some friends, and food to share.

Glass bottles

Reuse wine bottles to hold dinner candles or hand-dipped tapered candles or to display single flowers. Keep the labels on if they are interesting; soak the bottles with black tea to make them appear aged. Fill wide-necked bottles with bunches of flowers, either fresh or paper. Decorate with ribbons, strings of secondhand beads, or raffia. Raffia is inexpensive, and it can be used to decorate everything from chairs to candlesticks.

Pots, jars, and tins

Large, clear-glass pots or jars filled with fir cones, fruit, pebbles, leaves, or sand can make interesting bases for either candles or flower displays. Some items can quite happily be immersed in water but others, such as fir cones, are best left dry.

Fill other containers with small plants or sweets. Flowers look charming arranged in tins or jam jars, and remember that the smaller the jar or vase and the narrower its neck, the fewer flowers you will need—which can also help to keep costs down.

Renting

Renting is often a more affordable alternative to buying. You can even rent smaller finishing touches, such as butterfly decorations and table numbers (see the Directory).

Fair-trade decorations

If you need to buy anything from farther afield, look for products bearing the FAIRTRADE mark, from paper flowers to hand-printed fabrics, festive baubles to storm lanterns. Search online ethical stores or fair-trade shops; you'll find our favorites in the Directory.

Inexpensive and gorgeous

Raw materials
* Vintage buttons
* Homemade wildflower paper
* Bunting made from scraps of fabric
* Secondhand tablecloths
* Recycled ribbons
* Big bunches of natural raffia

Pots and jars
* Vintage terra-cotta
* Coir pots
* Tin cans
* Glass jam jars
* Wooden bowls
* Vintage cocktail glasses
* Sundae dishes
* Wide-necked bottles

Fair-trade ideas
* Wire card holders
* Tea-light holders
* Hand-printed napkins
* Strings of paper flowers
* Hand-sculpted ornaments
* Plant-wax candles
* Handmade paper cards

Creative lighting

Lighting is important as it helps to establish a special atmosphere. Candlelight and lanterns are warm and flattering, and both create a romantic ambience perfect for weddings.

Jam jars and hand-blown lanterns

Jam-jar lanterns are a thrifty yet pretty adornment. Collect jam or chutney jars in the weeks leading up to your wedding and wrap salvaged wire around the necks. Bend a hoop of wire over the tops and either leave them as they are or decorate them with a ribbon. They look magical hung from trees or on beaches.

Hand-blown, fine, recycled-glass lanterns can be used to decorate tables and to line pathways. Or, try filling them with water and using them as vases for a pretty, hanging flower display.

Tin-can candles

Following the method on page 164, fill an old food tin halfway with plant wax and leave it to cool completely. To create a lantern effect, punch a few holes in the sides of the tin, above the level of the candle, using a bradawl and small hammer. Add a wire hook if needed.

Pumpkin lanterns

For a memorable and quirky seasonal decoration, carve pumpkins into intricate butterfly- or flower-pattern lanterns, and place them in the centers of tthe ables or in hidden corners indoors or outside.

Vintage candlesticks

From Victoriana glass to antique silver, candlesticks can dress any table or display. Collect clear-glass candlesticks in different sizes, and arrange them in groups of odd numbers, such as threes or fives, in the centers of the tables. Or, try alternating short and tall candlesticks between vases of flowers. Use dinner candles made from plant-based waxes fragranced with essential oils, but be careful not to place candlesticks near open windows or drafts, as the breeze will make the candles drip and burn more quickly.

Candelabras

Stylish and graceful, candelabras always suit formal weddings. Decorate them with flowers, as shown on the opposite page, or leave them unadorned and light cream-colored, plant-wax candles for elegant simplicity. Look for antique or vintage candelabras, perhaps borrowed from friends, or rent them from a good rental company.

Ecofriendly candles

Regular candles are petroleum based and usually have synthetic fragrances. They can give off smoke and toxic chemicals as they burn. Instead, choose clean-burning candles made entirely from plant wax. Candles that are naturally fragranced with pure essential oils smell wonderful and can have therapeutic benefits, too.

Beeswax candles

Long-burning beeswax candles smell divine. They are available as either poured, container candles or hand rolled from sheets; try to buy those made from organic beeswax, and look for kits containing everything you need to create your own rolled dinner candles. (Remember that beeswax is not a vegan product.)

Tea lights

Plant-wax tea lights are delightful, creamy little candles. They tend to burn for considerably longer than regular tea lights and are often made from soy wax. Soya is a cash crop, and sometimes protected rain forest is destroyed in order to plant it. So look for candles made from sustainably farmed soy, produced without such deforestation.

A feast of homemade favors

Favors are traditionally given as thank-you tokens to guests for attending your wedding. From heavenly chocolates to personalized cards, you can make all manner of gifts that will please your family and friends, young and old. Think of unusual options that say something about you as a couple. I recently attended a wedding in Wales where they gave minipackets of Welsh cakes (a traditional type of fruit drop scone).

Truffles

Decadent little rounds of soft chocolate, dusted with fine, fair-trade cocoa powder, melt-in-the-mouth truffles are simple to make at home. Prepare them just a few days beforehand, and keep them cool.

Homemade sugared almonds

Five sugared almonds is the original favor given to symbolize wealth, happiness, health, long life, and fertility. But rather than buying preservative-laden store varieties, try cooking your own caramel-scented sweets with fair-trade organic almonds.

Heart biscuits

Delicious butter biscuits are a cost-effective treat. Use a heart-shaped cookie cutter, and pack the cookies into biodegradable cellophane bags tied with a natural raffia bow. For extra decoration, add colored icing and a dusting of edible sparkle. For a Christmas wedding, choose a holly- or tree-shaped cookie cutter, and pierce holes at the tops of the biscuits before baking. Once cooled, thread with ribbons so they double as tree decorations.

Favor boxes

Tiny decorative boxes are extremely popular to hold gifts, from trinkets to flower bulbs. Mass-produced boxes may have traveled many miles, so make your own, or buy boxes made from recycled or handmade paper and those bearing the FAIRTRADE mark. The most ecofriendly favor boxes are plantable ones made from wildflower-seed paper (see page 94), which can be planted in guests' gardens after the wedding. Look online for templates, and opt for a design in one piece, like the box above, rather than with a separate lid. These require less paper and are easier to make.

Seeds

Wrap organic seed packets in paper sleeves, hand-printed with details of your wedding. For a surprise, decant the seeds into handmade paper envelopes decorated with a vintage card and tied with a plush ribbon (remember to include planting instructions).

Lavender bags

Gorgeous, scented lavender bags are easy to sew and thrifty. For each bag, cut two heart shapes from a reclaimed fabric, preferably one with a small pattern. With right sides facing out, fill the center with dried, organic lavender flowers and topstitch neatly all the way around, three-quarters of inch in from the edge, by machine or hand. Carefully trim the edges with pinking shears; finish with a ribbon loop, fixed in place with a vintage button.

Paper scrolls

Combine place cards and favors by writing the table names or numbers, together with personal messages, on small pieces of handmade paper. Roll them into scrolls and display in alphabetical groups in terra-cotta pots or glass vases.

Natural Beauty

The best beauty preparations for a bride-to-be are a good skin-care regime and plenty of relaxation. I've been using and learning about natural products for many years now and am delighted whenever I can pass on what I've discovered to my friends and brides. As well as delicious skin-care brands and secrets, I've included some simple relaxation techniques and pampering treats. Enjoy them as you get ready for your big day and as part of your future lifestyle.

Ingredients to avoid

Parabens, mineral oils, synthetics, sulphates,
SLS, silicones, nano particles, GMOs, phthalates,
carbomers, DEAs, artificial colors, and animal-
tested ingredients. See the Glossary on page 215.

Organic skin care

Natural and organic skin care is increasingly popular, and a regimen based on plant products will contain fewer man-made chemicals, a number of which can trigger allergies. From the simplest range for sensitive skin to cutting-edge, plant-based brands, there is a solution for every bride (and groom). If you are changing from a synthetic product, give your skin a few weeks to adjust. You may get some blemishes at first, but drink lots of water and persevere—your skin will thank you for it.

Creams made from vegetable oils, fruit and nut oils, nut butters, and beeswax, fragranced only with pure essential oils, are good for the planet as well as your skin. You can find out more, including skin-care recipes, from *The Green Beauty Bible* by Sarah Stacey and Josephine Fairley, and *Natural Health and Body Care* and *Recipes for Natural Beauty*, both from Neal's Yard Remedies.

Why choose nonsynthetic?

The skin is the largest organ of the human body, and a significant percentage of what you apply to it is absorbed into your bloodstream. Most standard skin-care products contain chemicals that are either synthetic or petroleum based, and studies have shown that a number of these ingredients can have a detrimental effect on skin health.

Some mainstream companies have realized that consumers are examining labels more closely and have removed parabens and SLS (sodium lauryl sulphate, a harsh degreasing detergent). Nonetheless, labeling can be deceptive: Some products marked "natural" or "plant-based" only contain a small proportion of ingredients derived from nature. The way to tell if a cream or lotion is really natural is by checking the ingredients list and looking for logos, such as the Soil Association, BDIH, Ecocert, OFC, and USDA. A few products in our Directory may contain tiny amounts of food-grade preservatives, but these have been included because of their otherwise outstanding environmental credentials.

Your natural essentials

Cleansers

Cream or oil-based cleansers, especially those with sesame or jojoba oil, are great for dry skin. Coconut-derived rinse-off cleansers suit normal to combination skin.

Toners

Try rose for sensitive skin, neroli for dry skin, and lavender for problematic skin. Atomizers will minimize cotton-wool waste.

Serums and elixirs

These advanced antiaging products, designed to plump fine lines and add radiance, use beneficial plant extracts that firm and tighten skin. Apply them sparingly under moisturizer.

Facial oils

A great alternative to day or night cream, these pure botanical oils leave skin nourished, not greasy.

Moisturizers

Fragranced only with essential oils, these protect against atmospheric pollution as well as hydrate the skin. Neroli and shea butter are good for dry skin and rose for dehydrated; frankincense has amazing antiaging effects.

Face masks

Apply once a week; clay based will unblock pores and cream based will enrich parched skin.

Exfoliators

Choose a fine-grained product with ingredients such as ground oats and seeds. Use twice a week to reveal healthy new skin.

Organic muslin cloths

These can be used to remove cleansers and masks and to gently exfoliate.

A naturally healthy glow

Makeup, like skin-care products, can also contain undesirable ingredients. Fortunately, natural cosmetic companies now offer us the same standard of color and coverage without the unnecessary chemicals. Formulations have improved, and products are available for all skin types and tones, from sparkly eye shadows to creamy organic lipsticks.

Look for brands that are pushing the boundaries, using recycled packaging and renewable energy in their production. We chose Elysambre (www.elysambre .com) for most of the bridal looks in this book. It offers refillable containers for all its cosmetics, which are both ecofriendly and superstylish. For more ideas, visit www. naturisimo.com or www.futurenatural.com, and see the Directory.

Getting the best from ecomakeup

* Apply an organic moisturizer to prime the skin for a natural mineral-based foundation.
* When using a matte lipstick, apply organic lip balm afterward to help it set and to minimize dry patches. Apply lip balm before lipstick for a sheer look.
* Natural mascara is not waterproof but will suit contact-lens wearers and is easy to remove.
* Curl eyelashes before applying mascara to make your eyes appear bigger and your lashes longer.
* Check your makeup from the side using a handheld mirror in daylight, to see the photographer's view.

Animal testing

It is widely acknowledged that it is not ethically acceptable to test either products or ingredients on animals, but unfortunately it still happens. Truly natural skin care companies only test their ranges on human volunteers. Vegan brides should check if products contain beeswax.

Blemishes

If you develop a pimple the night before the wedding, cleanse your face, pat it dry with a clean towel, and apply tea tree essential oil to the blemish with a cotton ball. Before bed, change your pillowcase for a clean one, as the used one could harbor blemish-creating bacteria. To reduce the chance of pimples before the big day, take these small steps:

* Drink plenty of water in the preceding months.
* Follow a balanced organic diet.
* Keep stress levels low.
* Change your pillowcases twice a week.
* Find a natural skin-care regimen that suits you and follow it religiously.
* Always remove makeup before bed.

Puffy eyes

If you wake up on your wedding day with puffy eyes, place either a slice of fresh organic cucumber or a cool, wet chamomile tea bag on each eye for five minutes.

Miracle creams

Fruit-acid face masks or oil-rich balms are the perfect prewedding skin savers (never use clay-based masks on the day). Simply apply on the morning of the wedding, following the instructions, for smooth, photo-ready skin. Follow with an antiwrinkle cream to help minimize the appearance of fine lines and to prep your face for makeup. My favorites are as follows:

❋ Logona Wrinkle Therapy Fluid: a miracle cream that erases lines before your very eyes

❋ Nude Skincare's Miracle Mask: so simple to use, with fantastic line-reducing results

❋ REN Glycolactic Skin Renewal Peel Mask: an exfoliating mask to improve skin tone and firmness

❋ Neal's Yard Remedies Wild Rose Beauty Balm: a fragrant balm that reduces fine lines, boosts radiance, and softens dry skin

Karen and Lee, of Lee Matthews Studio, have created striking hair and makeup styles for this book.

Be stress free

Wedding planning can be stressful, however organized you are. I've included these relaxing tips to help keep your stress levels down and your energy high. Allow yourself an hour a week to unwind and to pamper your body and soul. Play soothing music and light candles to create a warm, calming atmosphere.

Aromatherapy oils

Essential oils extracted from plants and flowers can balance, relax, or energize. You can use them in an oil burner, in the bath, or for massage. All these methods can have positive effects on the senses and the skin. Never apply them directly to the skin (except for tea tree oil on pimples, see page 176); always dilute them first in a carrier such as almond oil. Pregnant women should consult an aromatherapist before using any essential oils.

Flower remedies

These are useful for emotional upset and stress. Bach Remedies are made from British flowers and Bush Remedies from Australian plants. The best known is Bach Rescue Remedy, a multipurpose remedy that is valuable after an accident, shock, or upset, and also for nerves. Carry it with you during the planning stage and on the wedding day, just in case. My favorite individual remedy is White Chestnut. This helps to quiet an active mind at night, when your thoughts are swimming with invitations and color schemes.

DIY spa treats

You can easily replicate many therapeutic spa treatments at home with a few simple ingredients. Look for oils, dried flowers, and herbs in natural beauty stores such as Neal's Yard Remedies. Try the ideas below with your groom, mom, or bridesmaids.

Facials

A monthly facial will improve the health of your skin and help it glow. First, apply cleanser and slowly massage it into the skin using small circular motions. Finish each circuit of the face with a gentle press on the temples. Once rinsed, apply a face mask, avoiding the eye area. Pop fresh slices of cooled cucumber over your eyes, sit back, and relax for ten minutes—enjoy a warm herbal tea for maximum therapeutic effect.

Remove the mask with a warm muslin cloth, and splash your face ten times with fresh, cold water to close the pores. Then, using a few drops of organic facial oil, gently massage, following the contours of the face. Finally, apply a small amount of eye gel or cream to the eye area using small patting motions with your ring finger.

Wedding planner tip:
To help essential oils to disperse in bath water, mix a few drops into a tablespoon of milk first.

Body scrub

For baby-soft skin, make a paste from three tablespoons of olive oil, a couple of drops of essential oil, a teaspoon of runny honey, and a handful of either sugar, salt, or coarse oats (avoid salt if you have sensitive skin). Rub the mixture lightly onto dry skin, paying attention to elbows but avoiding the face. Rinse off with warm water and pat your skin dry. Follow with a rich organic body cream or oil.

Bath soak

For a relaxing and skin-softening bath, place a handful each of oats, dried marigolds, and lavender or rose petals in a muslin cloth. Tie the cloth into a ball and plac it e under the hot tap while you run the bath. Let the herbs infuse in the water and add a tablespoon of shea butter.

And breathe . . .

If you are about to make a speech or walk down the aisle and are feeling a little anxious, take three deep breaths. This will help you to relax and give you a confidence boost. Similarly, if you are having difficulty sleeping and switching off, concentrate and breathe in gently for a count of seven, then breathe out for a count of eleven. Repeat until you feel more relaxed.

Stress-busting essential oils

❋ Chamomile: a heavenly scent, and deeply relaxing. Blend with lavender and rose in a bath before bedtime for a good night's sleep.

❋ Geranium: a balancing oil, useful when you feel out of sorts. Blend with rose to enhance your mood.

❋ Jasmine: When things get tough, choose sweet-smelling jasmine to bring a sense of renewed optimism.

❋ Rose: If you feel weepy from emotional stress, the scent of rose can help keep tears at bay. Plus, it smells divine.

Edible face masks

These face and hand treatments are all made using ingredients found in your fridge, garden, or greengrocery. Choose organic fruits to minimize exposure to pesticides. Afterward, relax with a lavender eye mask.

STRAWBERRY EXFOLIATING MASK

1 tomato

3 strawberries

1 teaspoon of manuka honey

Chop the tomato finely and mash with the strawberries and honey. Apply to damp skin, avoiding the eye area, and leave for 5 minutes. Rinse well and moisturize for silky-smooth, decongested skin.

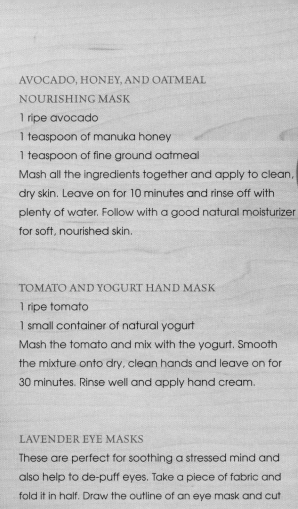

AVOCADO, HONEY, AND OATMEAL NOURISHING MASK

1 ripe avocado
1 teaspoon of manuka honey
1 teaspoon of fine ground oatmeal

Mash all the ingredients together and apply to clean, dry skin. Leave on for 10 minutes and rinse off with plenty of water. Follow with a good natural moisturizer for soft, nourished skin.

TOMATO AND YOGURT HAND MASK

1 ripe tomato
1 small container of natural yogurt

Mash the tomato and mix with the yogurt. Smooth the mixture onto dry, clean hands and leave on for 30 minutes. Rinse well and apply hand cream.

LAVENDER EYE MASKS

These are perfect for soothing a stressed mind and also help to de-puff eyes. Take a piece of fabric and fold it in half. Draw the outline of an eye mask and cut it out so that you have two identical pieces. With right sides facing inward, carefully stitch all the way around the edges, leaving a small hole about three-quarters of an inch long. Turn the bag inside out and fill it with dried lavender flowers. Sew up the hole and stitch a wide ribbon onto each side seam as a tie. Lie back, place the mask over your eyes, and relax.

Hair and finishing touches

Organic natural shampoos, conditioners, hair masks, and styling products now rival mainstream brands and keep your hair and scalp healthy without synthetic chemicals. Choose your wedding-day hairstyle with your dress in mind. With a floaty 1970s chiffon dress, flowing locks and a simple hair band around the forehead are perfect, or try a daisy chain with long dresses that have simple lines. Structured modern gowns favor an amazing updo, while vintage skirt-suits look stunning with short hair. Pretty antique tiaras and homemade flower corsages complement almost every style and can lift a look with minimal effort.

For shiny, conditioned hair, work in a tablespoon of pure coconut oil, wrap your hair up in a towel, and leave for an hour. Then massage unscented shampoo into the hair before adding water to create a lather. Rinse with plenty of warm water, and dry as normal.

Teeth and tans

Book a dental checkup at least a month before the wedding, to allow enough time for any work you may need. Rather than having teeth chemically whitened, make a "clean and polish" appointment with a hygienist three days before your wedding.

Fake tans have become a popular preparation for the big day. You can now find natural fake tans in both cream and spray applications. Exfoliating thoroughly beforehand and moisturizing well afterward will help them last.

Nails

Most nail polishes contain toxic chemicals such as formaldehyde. A few companies have developed kinder alternatives, in fabulous colors such as vintage rose and hot pink. Either choose a brand such as Zoya or Butter London—which are toluene, formaldehyde, and DBP free—or, alternatively, shine your nails with a buffing board for an elegant look without polish.

Natural perfumes

Scents are notorious for containing many synthetic chemicals. Happily, companies such as Jo Wood Organics are producing organic eaux de toilette, while Florascent uses natural essences. Robert Tisserand's *The Art of Aromatherapy* tells you how to make flower waters (my tip is to put flower water in an atomizer with a drop of essential oil from the same flower to accentuate the scent).

Time out for the two of you

It is important that you and your groom have time for each other in the weeks leading up to the big day. In the final weeks, a wedding can become time-consuming, so my advice is that you take at least a day off each week to relax and enjoy each other's company, with no mention of the wedding. This ensures that you remain focused on why you are marrying and don't exhaust yourselves.

Beauty must-haves for the big day

❉ DIY mineral-water spray—decant local mineral water into a small bottle with an atomizer top. Use during the day to refresh skin; it also helps to "set" makeup.

❉ Small makeup kit containing natural lipstick, lip balm, and powder.

❉ Organic blotting tissues to keep shine under control.

❉ A small deodorant stone (available from health-food stores and natural pharmacies). These leave no stains and are completely natural.

❉ Aloe vera gel. In summer, arm yourself with a parasol to keep shaded, but if your skin is exposed to the sun, aloe will soothe it and reduce redness.

Top DIY hair tips

❋ Make your own salt spray by dissolving sea salt in boiled water. Spray onto damp hair and style for a tousled, fashionable matte finish. Ideal for a beach wedding.

❋ Decorate your hair with small fresh flowers (your florist can provide these on clips). Alternatively, try tiny vintage corsages and fine hair bands for 1950s chic.

❋ Be comfortable on the day. If you usually wear your hair loose, don't feel pressured to have it up.

❋ If you are home-styling your hair, have a couple of trial runs and take photographs from the front, side, and back to remind you of what works.

❋ Choose a natural, nonaerosol hairspray to set your updo.

Lee has used hellebores to dress Karen's hair. Hand-finished couture silk gown by Jessica Charleston.

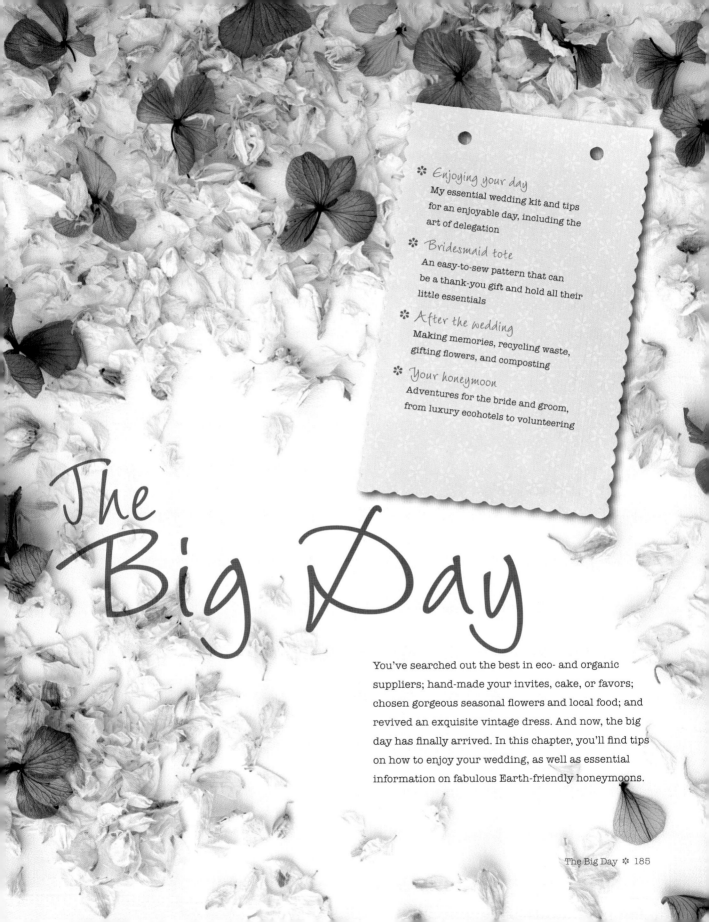

* *Enjoying your day*
  My essential wedding kit and tips
  for an enjoyable day, including the
  art of delegation

* *Bridesmaid tote*
  An easy-to-sew pattern that can
  be a thank-you gift and hold all their
  little essentials

* *After the wedding*
  Making memories, recycling waste,
  gifting flowers, and composting

* *Your honeymoon*
  Adventures for the bride and groom,
  from luxury ecohotels to volunteering

The Big Day

You've searched out the best in eco- and organic
suppliers; hand-made your invites, cake, or favors;
chosen gorgeous seasonal flowers and local food; and
revived an exquisite vintage dress. And now, the big
day has finally arrived. In this chapter, you'll find tips
on how to enjoy your wedding, as well as essential
information on fabulous Earth-friendly honeymoons.

Enjoying your day

*P*lanning a wedding is time-consuming and requires considerable effort. You may have spent months, even years, preparing for your perfect big day and carefully choosing your green products and services. And the bulk of this work usually falls on the bride. The result is a day to which a great deal of expectation is attached.

The anticipation of a wedding can be delightful but can also bring stress and worry. In my experience, the best advice I can give to brides is to relax on the day and go with the flow. Small things may go wrong—a guest might be late or you may stain your dress— but these tiny annoyances are unimportant. The reason you are holding a wedding is to be married; the party is a nice aside. So be happy, smile, relax into your day, and enjoy every minute, as it will fly by in no time.

Keep your sense of humor

A bride once called me the day before her wedding in an absolute panic. She was beside herself: Something terrible had happened, and she had no idea what to do. "Louise, you have to help me," she pleaded.

It turned out that her dog had eaten all her artisanal chocolate favors, handmade boxes and all. This bride was a lifelong friend, so I instantly knew what to do: I laughed. And the minute I laughed, so did she. In that moment, she realized that it wasn't the end of the world; it wouldn't stop the wedding. New favors were made, the guests loved the story, and we still laugh about it to this day.

Delegation

On-the-day delegation is an important part of wedding planning. If you are employing the services of an ecowedding planner, you won't need to do this, but if not, it helps to have friends on standby for specific tasks. Write each person a list so that he or she understands what is required. If responsible for checking that vendors have arrived, make sure that the person has the correct contact details.

Husband and wife

After the ceremony, try to have at least ten minutes alone together, away from the hustle and bustle of the party. You will be entertaining your guests for the rest of the day so pencil in time that is just for the two of you.

Inclement weather

Be prepared and take a golfing umbrella and Wellies. Wind and rain can, however, make for dramatic outdoor photos—bride and groom under an umbrella with veil flying in the breeze. If you laugh about it, you will feel much better.

My essential, natural wedding-day kit

I would recommend that you pack a little bag, well in advance of the day, containing these essentials. It is surprising how useful they can be!

- ❋ Bach Rescue Remedy or Bush Flower SOS remedy
- ❋ A natural headache remedy
- ❋ Traveler's first-aid kit, including bandages
- ❋ Safety pins
- ❋ Pocket sewing kit, including thread that matches your dress
- ❋ Chalk to cover marks on your dress
- ❋ Small ball of natural string or twine
- ❋ Scissors
- ❋ Organic flannel
- ❋ Matches
- ❋ Some essential items of natural makeup—lip balm, mascara, powder
- ❋ Packet of FSC or recycled tissues, or a handkerchief
- ❋ Hair pins that match your hair color
- ❋ A golfing umbrella, preferably a white one, or a paper parasol in high summer, to protect you from rain or sun

Wedding planner tip:
Remember to talk to your groom! It is easy
to spend all of your time speaking with your
guests instead, but remember it is your day.

Bridesmaid tote

This tote is a great thank-you gift and can be made with any fabrics you have on hand. It looks pretty with a complementary, paler lining. Fill with on-the-day essentials to make bridesmaids feel appreciated.

YOU WILL NEED:

2 pieces of fabric, at least 1¼ x 3 feet each

A piece of fabric 3¼ feet x 6¼ inches, for the handle

Measuring tape, tailor's chalk, and fabric scissors

Ribbons and lace

Vintage buttons

Needle, pins, and matching thread

Sewing machine (not essential)

METHOD:

1. Draw 4 rectangles measuring 1¼ x 1½ feet on your material—2 on each pattern of fabric, if you are using a different lining material. Cut them out.

2. Take the piece that will be the outside front and stitch ribbons and lace on top to make a design (see the photograph on the opposite page).

3. Pin the front and back outside pieces together, right sides facing inward, and stitch along three sides to form a bag shape.

4. Repeat with the two lining pieces, this time leaving a 2-inch gap in the seam.

5. Pinch out the bottom two corners of the outer bag, and stitch horizontally across each corner to form an equal triangle. Repeat with the lining bag.

6. Cut 2 more pieces of fabric, 3¼ feet long and 3 inch wide, for the handle. Pin them together, right sides inward, and stitch down each long side. Turn the handle right side out.

7. Turn the outer layer of the bag right side out, and place it inside the lining so that the right sides of the fabric face each other.

8. Tuck the handle in between the bags so it falls in a loop at the bottom, and line up the edges of the handle between the raw seams on each side.

9. Stitch together at the top edge, all the way around.

10. Turn the bag right side out by pulling all the fabric, including the handle, through the hole in the lining.

11. Sew up the hole, pushing the lining back down into the outer bag, and shake.

12. Embellish with a pin-on corsage (see page 68).

> **Wedding planner tip:**
> Press the seams as you go along for a crisp, professional finish, then lightly press the whole bag at the end.

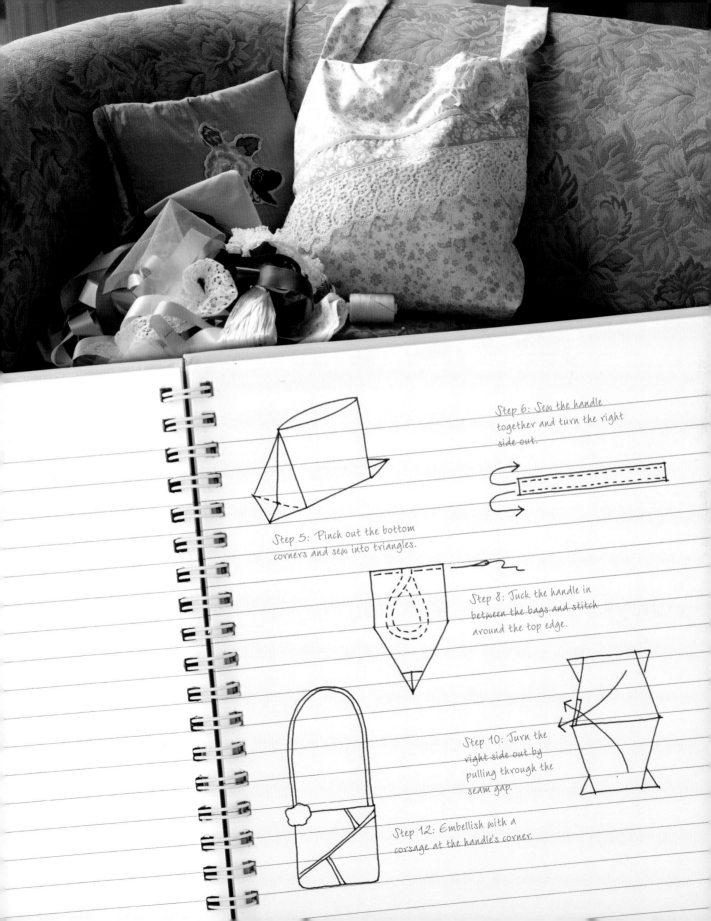

Step 6: Sew the handle together and turn the right side out.

Step 5: Pinch out the bottom corners and sew into triangles.

Step 8: Tuck the handle in between the bags and stitch around the top edge.

Step 10: Turn the right side out by pulling through the seam gap.

Step 12: Embellish with a corsage at the handle's corner.

After the wedding

It is a fashionable custom to leave your reception before it ends and go straight to the honeymoon. Whether it's a snug bed-and-breakfast a mile down the road or a train ride to somewhere you've never explored, it is fun to dress for the occasion. If you love vintage, why not invest in an original 1950s frock and vanity case for your trip, and enjoy filling the case with natural and organic treats?

Wedding memories

Keep tokens from your day as mementos and gather them into an antique box or handmade album. A pressed flower from your bouquet, place card, bottle label or cork, pebble, dried leaf, program, handful of confetti, and speeches can all be saved and enjoyed for years to come.

The postparty cleanup

Delegate post-party tasks to your good friends, so that you don't have to worry. Here are a few tips to get them started:

❈ Provide marked recycling bins for paper, cans, food waste, and plastics.

❈ Try to use cardboard boxes or biodegradable cornstarch bags to collect waste.

❈ Collect any spare toys, games, and nonperishable favors, and take them to a local thrift store.

❈ To make distribution of floral displays easy, write notes on the place cards of the guests you would like them to go to, so that they can take them home. Alternatively, hold a raffle using the place cards.

❈ Ask the venue managers if there is a compost bin for food and floral waste.

❈ If you are having a beach, park, or garden wedding, ask a few friends to pick up litter to ensure that you don't leave any trace.

❈ Allocate one person to oversee the return of rented items, such as furniture and suits, the following day.

> ### Good morning!
> If you and your guests are staying the night, continue the celebrations the following morning with a big, organic breakfast. Make the most of a Kåta tepee or yurt by eating together inside before the tent is dismantled.

Your honeymoon

The choice of eco-aware honeymoon possibilities is endless, whether volunteering in Eastern Europe or luxuriating at an ecospa. Consider "slow" travel and ethical options to minimize your impact.

Organic bed-and-breakfasts and ecohotels

Think about staying close to home. You can find environmentally aware and organic bed-and-breakfast retreats for many countries in *Alastair Sawday's Green Places to Stay* (www.sawdays.co.uk). Spend a day beachcombing, then head back for dinner in front of a log fire. Sample delicious local breakfasts and natural toiletries while wrapped in an organic cotton bathrobe.

For luxurious organic spa days and Michelin-starred food, try an ecohotel from one of the sites listed in the Directory, with gorgeous natural furnishings and modern green gadgets.

Honeymooning on a shoestring

Backpacking, hiking, house-swapping, camping—you can have a dream holiday and spend very little. If you crave luxury, book a weekend in an ecoboutique hotel. Alternatively, many organic farms now have permanent yurt fields, with proper beds and warm blankets. Zac and I spent a fabulous shoestring break in Venice, camping at Marina de Venezia, next to miles of sandy private beach. By day, we took the boat across to Venice; in the evenings, we barbecued at the campsite and watched the sun go down together.

Festivals

These can offer distinctive accommodation as well as music and atmosphere. Glastonbury, for example, has private tepees in the festival fields or luxurious shikar tents on the outskirts, complete with butlers and a private bar. Festivals are held across the globe; choosing one local to you will help to reduce your carbon footprint.

Ecotourism

You may have been dreaming about and saving for your honeymoon for years, and looking forward to relaxing and exploring somewhere different. There are many ecofriendly options worldwide, from safari lodges in Africa to snorkeling in tropical blue seas. Avoid large chain hotels and, instead, choose local independents who work hard to protect the environment and benefit their neighboring society. Visit www.ecotourism.org for more information.

Slow travel

Go slow and choose more sustainable transport, such as bus, train, and passenger boat. Not only will you use less carbon, you will see more of the country. If you have to go by air, then offset your flight through a reputable carbon-offset program.

Volunteering holidays

Adventurous couples could go on a volunteering holiday. Companies offer expeditions across the globe to carry out important conservation work. Whether restoring forests in Cameroon, repairing mountain trails in Iceland, or building nesting sites for wild birds in Bulgaria, you will have fun while helping the environment.

Wedding planner tip:
Pack lavender essential oil to treat mosquito bites, citronella oil to repel insects, and aloe vera gel to soothe sun-exposed skin.

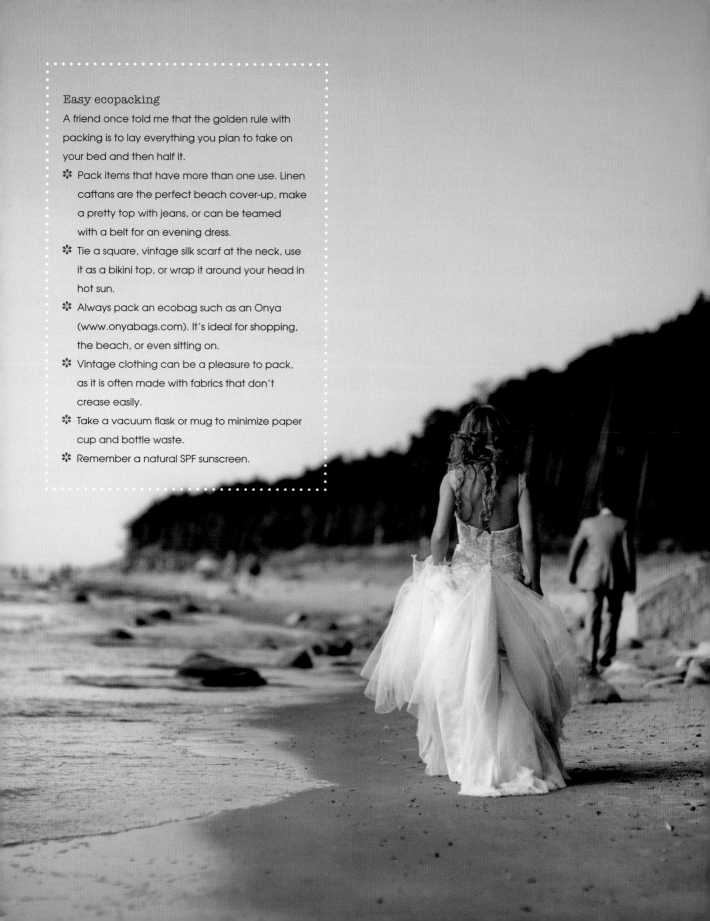

Easy ecopacking

A friend once told me that the golden rule with packing is to lay everything you plan to take on your bed and then half it.

❋ Pack items that have more than one use. Linen caftans are the perfect beach cover-up, make a pretty top with jeans, or can be teamed with a belt for an evening dress.

❋ Tie a square, vintage silk scarf at the neck, use it as a bikini top, or wrap it around your head in hot sun.

❋ Always pack an ecobag such as an Onya (www.onyabags.com). It's ideal for shopping, the beach, or even sitting on.

❋ Vintage clothing can be a pleasure to pack, as it is often made with fabrics that don't crease easily.

❋ Take a vacuum flask or mug to minimize paper cup and bottle waste.

❋ Remember a natural SPF sunscreen.

Natural Wedding Planner

This planner is based on the main stages of organizing your wedding, rather than on a specific timeline. Some couples may have years to plan their wedding, while others may only have a few weeks. You may not need all of the elements below—many will only apply to larger weddings—so simply choose those which are relevant, and check them off as they are done.

Stage 1: The exciting bit

This stage can take as long as you want it to. But remember that some popular venues and churches need to be booked well in advance.

Start compiling your wedding notebook (never too early) with ideas for your natural day (see page 32). ☐

Choose your wedding date. ☐

Decide the type of ceremony you would like to have (see page 30). ☐

Consider how many guests will attend. ☐

Research seasonal flowers and produce available at the time of your wedding (see the seasonal calendars on pages 216 and 217). ☐

Select and book the venue for your ceremony (if required, meet with the rabbi, vicar, priest, or minister). ☐

Select and book the venue for your reception (after visiting different options). ☐

Choose your best man and maid of honor, if appropriate. ☐

Rent a tepee or tent and furniture. ☐

Buy wedding insurance, if it will be a large wedding. ☐

Decide on your wedding registry. ☐

Make wildflower-seed paper for invites, decorations, and favor boxes (see page 94). ☐

Order or make your invitations. ☐

Launch your wedding Web site. ☐

Send out invitations or e-vites. ☐

Start your natural skin-care regimen. ☐

Stage 2: Bride and groom

Enjoy spending time with your groom on these elements—they are all the personal aspects of your day.

Shop for or make your dress. ☐

Find your bridal accessories and make your dress corsage (see page 68). ☐

Book your honeymoon (if you need your passports, make sure they are valid). ☐

Book first-night accommodation (if you are not going straight to your honeymoon or staying at the venue). ☐

Choose your groom's outfit. ☐

Find accessories for the groom. ☐

Shop for wedding rings, or have an existing ring reworked (see page 79). ☐

Sew your wedding-day bag (see page 88). ☐

Choose your first dance song. ☐

Discuss the ceremony music, hymns, vows, poetry, and readings. ☐

Stage 3: Vendors

Some vendors get booked up quickly, especially photographers. If you are planning on a handmade or DIY day, this stage might take a little longer.

Book a photographer and discuss the shots you would like. ☐

Book a DJ or compile your iPod playlist and/or hire musicians. ☐

Book hair and makeup appointments or decide on a style to do yourself. ☐

Book a caterer or decide on your own homemade menu. ☐

Make chutneys a few weeks beforehand, so that they can mature (see page 114). ☐

Rent crockery, cutlery, and serving dishes, if required. ☐

Collect baskets and crates to transport food, if required. ☐

Book a florist or attend a floristry workshop. ☐

Book transport—rickshaws, buses, or tandems—if required. ☐

Stage 4: Guests

Bear in mind that set seating plans can take a long time to finalize.

Find bridesmaids' outfits. ☐

Draw up the final guest list. ☐

Design the seating layout, if required. ☐

Finalize guest numbers with caterers or calculate food requirements
if making your own food. ☐

Arrange guests' camping fields or other accommodation. ☐

Sew bridesmaids' tote bags and fill with handmade gifts (see page 188). ☐

Make gifts for family and friends. ☐

Stage 5: Decor and details

The length of time to allow for this stage depends on whether you are buying eco-,
vintage, and fair-trade decorations, or making your own.

Create or find chair or pew decorations (see page 50),
bunting, and other venue decorations. ☐

Make teacup candles, if required (see page 164). ☐

Make favors for each guest. ☐

Make or order place cards (plus a few extras, just in case). ☐

Order the cake from a baker or ask a friend or relative (if you are making
your own, have a trial run). ☐

Enjoy your bachelor and bachelorette celebrations, whether separate or joint. ☐

Have a dental checkup. ☐

Write down a list of friends' duties for recycling after the reception. ☐

Choose one or two friends to supervise the cleanup, and book necessary rental
company collections after the day. ☐

Give the best man and maid of honor the telephone numbers of all vendors. ☐

Have a makeup and hair trial, whether professional or at home. ☐

Make or have printed the menus and other on-the-day stationery (see page 103). ☐

Put all your decorations into boxes or crates labeled with the contents. ☐

Stage 6: The week before

It's important to set aside time to relax during this stage, so that you don't burn out.

Haircuts for bride and groom. ☐

Write speeches. ☐

Final dress fitting, if necessary. ☐

Break in your shoes. ☐

Order your flowers, if not using a florist. ☐

Check that you have something, old, new, borrowed, and blue. ☐

Bake your own cake or cupcakes (see pages 124 and 128). ☐

Prepare your own food with family and friends. ☐

Pack your wedding-day kit (see page 186). ☐

Pack your honeymoon bags (remember your passport). ☐

Confirm all vendors by telephone. ☐

Tell the best man which vendors need to be paid in cash on the day,
and give him the correct amount of money in labeled envelopes. ☐

Stage 7: The day before

If it is a hot day, remember to keep out of the sun to avoid tan lines or burning.

Decorate the tent or venue with friends and family. ☐

Tie your bridal bouquet, if you are making it yourself—keep it somewhere
cool and dark. ☐

Ask a friend to transport your cake, if homemade, to the venue. ☐

Give yourself a home manicure. ☐

Enjoy a relaxed dinner with friends. ☐

Wash your hair. ☐

Add any extras to your wedding-day kit, such as your speech or family gifts. ☐

Give your bridesmaids their thank-you tote bags filled with
little handmade gifts and treats. ☐

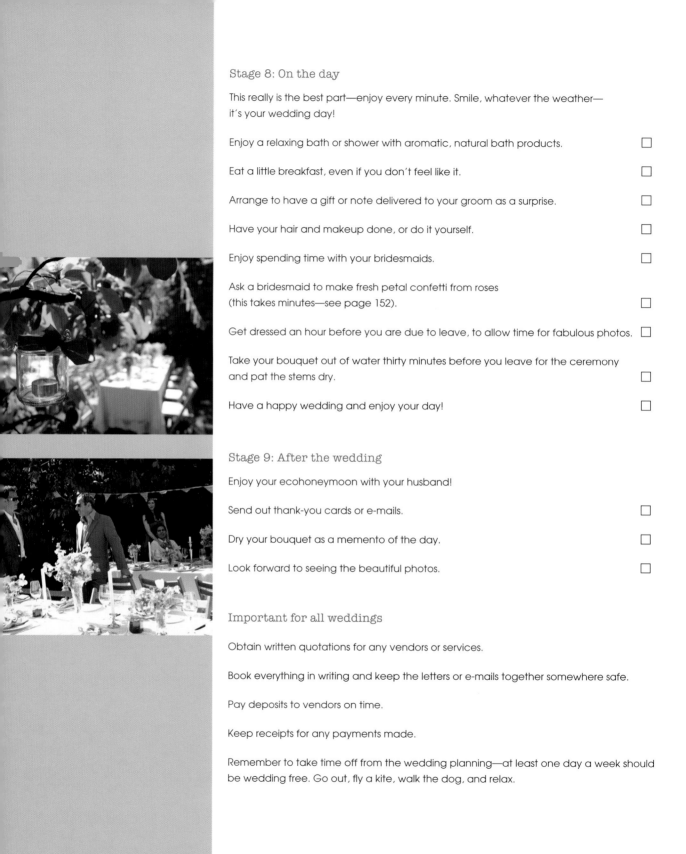

Stage 8: On the day

This really is the best part—enjoy every minute. Smile, whatever the weather—
it's your wedding day!

Enjoy a relaxing bath or shower with aromatic, natural bath products. ☐

Eat a little breakfast, even if you don't feel like it. ☐

Arrange to have a gift or note delivered to your groom as a surprise. ☐

Have your hair and makeup done, or do it yourself. ☐

Enjoy spending time with your bridesmaids. ☐

Ask a bridesmaid to make fresh petal confetti from roses
(this takes minutes—see page 152). ☐

Get dressed an hour before you are due to leave, to allow time for fabulous photos. ☐

Take your bouquet out of water thirty minutes before you leave for the ceremony
and pat the stems dry. ☐

Have a happy wedding and enjoy your day! ☐

Stage 9: After the wedding

Enjoy your ecohoneymoon with your husband!

Send out thank-you cards or e-mails. ☐

Dry your bouquet as a memento of the day. ☐

Look forward to seeing the beautiful photos. ☐

Important for all weddings

Obtain written quotations for any vendors or services.

Book everything in writing and keep the letters or e-mails together somewhere safe.

Pay deposits to vendors on time.

Keep receipts for any payments made.

Remember to take time off from the wedding planning—at least one day a week should
be wedding free. Go out, fly a kite, walk the dog, and relax.

This is a selection of my favorite books for natural-wedding reading. Some of them relate to weddings and honeymoons and some do not, but all are useful and interesting to leaf through, look at, and keep by for tips.

Venue and travel guides

The Alastair Sawday guides:
Eat Slow Britain
Go Slow England
Green Places to Stay
Special Places: Venues in Britain

Eco Hotels of the World, Alex Conti
Ecoescape: Responsible Escapism in the UK,
    Laura Burgess
The Guardian Green Travel Guide, edited by Liane Katz
Organic Places to Stay, Linda Moss

Cooking, growing, and picking your own

Cake Chic, Peggy Porschen
Cakes for Romantic Occasions,
    May Clee-Cadman
The Complete Gardener, Monty Don
The Dairy Book of Family Cookery, Alexandra Artley
Encyclopedia of Organic Gardening, HDRA
*Favourite Country Preserves: Traditional Home-made
    Jam, Chutney and Pickle Recipes*, Carol Wilson
Flower Course, Jane Packer
*The Forager Handbook: A Guide to the Edible Plants
    of Britain*, Miles Irving
*How to Store Your Garden Produce: The Key to
    Self-Sufficiency*, Piers Warren and Tessa Pettingell
The International Book of Sugarcraft (books 1 and 2),
    Nicholas Lodge and Janice Murfitt
Jekka's Complete Herb Book, Jekka McVicar
The Little Book of Organic Farming,
    The Soil Association
Seasonal Preserves, Joanna Farrow
Seasonal Wreaths and Bouquets, Paula Pryke
Sugar Flowers for Cake Decorating, Alan Dunn
Your Organic Allotment, Pauline Pears and Ian Spence

Handmade and DIY

Creative Handmade Paper, David Watson
Knitting in No Time, Melody Griffiths
Loop Pretty Knits, Susan Cropper
Papermaking with Garden Plants and Common Weeds,
    Helen Heibert

*Printing by Hand: A Modern Guide to Printing with
    Handmade Stamps, Stencils, and Silk Screens*,
    Lena Corwin
*Sew It Up: A Modern Manual of Practical and Decorative
    Sewing Techniques*, Ruth Singer
Wedding Invitations, Jennifer Cegielski

Vintage and shopping

*Alligators, Old Mink and New Money:
    One Woman's Adventures in Vintage Clothing*,
    Alison Houtte and Melissa Houtte
It's Vintage, Darling!: How to Be a Clothes Connoisseur,
    Christa Weil
*The Little Guide to Vintage Shopping: Insider Tips,
    Helpful Hints, Hip Shops*, Melody Fortier
*Making Vintage Bags: 20 Original Sewing Patterns for
    Vintage Bags and Purses*, Emma Brennan
The Rough Guide to Ethical Shopping,
    Duncan Clark
*Secondhand Chic: Finding Fabulous Fashion at
    Consignment, Vintage, and Thrift Stores*, Christa Weil
*Shopping for Vintage: The Definitive
    Guide to Vintage Fashion*, Funmi Odulate
*Vintage Fashion: Collecting and Wearing Designer
    Classics*, Carlton Books
Vintage Handbags, Marnie Fogg
Vintage Shoes, Caroline Cox

Natural beauty

The Art of Aromatherapy, Robert B. Tisserand
The Green Beauty Bible, Sarah Stacey and
    Josephine Fairley
Natural Health and Body Care,
    Neal's Yard Remedies
The Practice of Aromatherapy, Dr. Jean Valnet
Recipes for Natural Beauty, Neal's Yard Remedies
Vogue Natural Health and Beauty, Bronwen Meredith

Eco, ethical, and thrifty

Ms. Harris's Book of Green Household Management,
    Caroline Harris
The Thrift Book, India Knight
What's in This Stuff?, Pat Thomas

Natural Wedding Directory

Officiants

www.weddingceremony.org
Find an officiant in your state.

Venues

www.audubonnaturalist.org
Marry in one of the society's properties
and support its education and
conservation programs.

www.barndiva.com
Weddings in the barn or vineyards in
California, with local and organic food.

www.business-services.upenn.edu
The Morris Arboretum is part of the
University of Pennsylvania.

www.dinegreen.com
Find green restaurants near you.

www.duckfarm.org
Langetree Duck Farm ecocenter, Texas.

www.elmontesagrado.com
Luxurious ecohotel and spa in Taos,
New Mexico, with its own natural
water recycling and sacred circle.

www.environmentallyfriendlyhotels
.com
Rated listings of green hotels by
city and state, showing the efforts they
are making, from renewable energy
to organic food.

www.greenalpacayurts.com
Yurt set in secluded woodland
in the New Hampshire countryside.

www.greenhotels.com
Web site of the Green
Hotels Association.

www.gwinnettehc.org
Environmental and heritage
center available for weddings and
celebrations in Georgia.

www.hawaiiislandretreat.com
Green boutique hotel, spa, and
yurt village on Big Island, with
ocean-view wedding locations
and organic catering.

www.heardmuseum.org
The Heard Natural Science Museum
and Wildlife Sanctuary, Texas, with
native plant garden and a striking
amphitheater.

www.herecomestheguide.com
Search for venues, including farms,
ranches, and beachside locations,
in California; Washington, DC; and
Chicago (check with individual venues
about their green credentials).

www.hotelhelix.com
Ecoboutique hotel in Washington, DC.

www.lfy.ca
Sale and rental of hand-built yurts
made from coppice wood in
Nova Scotia.

www.littlestsimonsisland.com
Conservation is key on Little
St. Simons Island, Georgia, which is
ideal for small weddings.

www.museumca.org/usa
Museums offer a different kind of venue.

www.nps.gov
The National Park Service Web site—
Yellowstone, Yosemite, and more all
over the United States.

www.nypl.org/spacerental
The New York Public Library is
a beautiful reception space.

www.stanfordinn.com
Including weddings in the organic
herb garden, with award-winning
vegetarian and vegan food,
in Mendocino, California.

www.tpforganics.com
Traders Point Creamery is an organic
dairy farm and restaurant near
Indianapolis, with contemporary
rustic interiors and gardens.

www.freewebs.com/wedsea
Mary Crook's selections of wedding
locations along the Oregon coast.

Green wedding Web sites

www.greenweddingshowcase.com
Mid-Atlantic green wedding show.

www.green-wedding.net
Site with green wedding products
available to buy online.

www.thenaturalweddingbook.com
The Web site of this book.

www.thenaturalweddingcompany
.co.uk
Site with advice and directory,
including US and Canadian suppliers.

Event planners and photographers

www.engagingaffairs.com
Eco-aware wedding planners in Washington, DC.

www.gorgeousandgreenevents.com
San Francisco–based green event planner; also has a boutique with recycled cards, upcycled jewelry, and more.

www.greenerphotography.org
Find green photographers in your area.

Wedding gowns

www.bridesagainstbreastcancer.org
Find gown sales across the country and support the Making Memories charity.

www.consciouselegance.com
Established, award-wining ecowedding gowns, based in Pennsylvania.

www.ebay.com
One-stop online auction site.

www.etsy.com/shop/lillipopsdesigns
Perfect ecofriendly outfits for flower girls.

www.fashion-era.com
Information site featuring vintage clothing and patterns.

www.freecycle.org
Source of dresses and accessories completely for free.

www.little-flowers.com
Environmentally friendly bridal gowns, bridesmaids' and flower girls' dresses.

www.lorimarsha.com
Unusual bridal gowns made from recycled fabrics and trimmings.

www.naturalbridals.com
Beautiful gowns made with sustainable fabrics, from Atlanta, Georgia.

www.preownedweddingdresses.com
Find your dream dress at this online boutique.

www.punkrockbride.com
Alternative wedding dresses made to order.

www.puridee.com
Gowns crafted using natural and ethical fabrics.

www.recapturedesigns.com
Restyled vintage gowns from a Berkeley, California, studio, and online accessories boutique.

www.recycledbride.com
Gently worn dresses and vintage jewelry online.

www.ruffleswap.com
Dress-swapping marketplace for lovers of fashion.

www.thecottonbride.com
Beautiful handmade dresses in cotton, linen, and silk.

www.thefrock.com
Online boutique of exquisite vintage bridal gowns.

www.thegartergirl.com
Gorgeous ecofriendly garters for your big day.

www.voguepatterns.com
Fabulous vintage *Vogue* patterns to buy online.

Accessories and groomswear

www.beyondskin.co.uk
Cruelty-free, vegan, handmade footwear, delivered worldwide.

www.junkystyling.co.uk
Fabulous menswear created by reworking vintage pieces, available in New York City.

www.magpievintage.co.uk
Vintage bags and accessories, delivered worldwide.

www.recapturedesigns.com
Vintage bridal accessories.

www.terraplana.com
Fabulous ethical shoes for any occasion.

www.urbanfoxeco.com
Ecofriendly lingerie company based in the Midwest.

www.vintagevixen.com
Camisoles, gloves, purses, and more from the twentieth century.

Rings and other jewelry

www.bario-neal.com
Hand-crafted jewelry with reclaimed materials and ethically sourced stones.

www.brilliantearth.com
Canadian diamond rings made with recycled gold and platinum.

www.greendivabridal.com
Ecofriendly, vintage, and fair-trade products.

www.happymangobeads.com
Recycled and hand-crafted beads, many fair trade.

www.kylerdesigns.com
Stylish, sustainable jewelry.

www.leblas.com
Jewelry made from recycled metals and conflict-free gems.

www.newyorkweddingring.com
Spend a day making your own wedding rings.

www.nodirtygold.org
Information on gold and unsustainable mining practices.

www.queensofvintage.com
Online zine for lovers of vintage everywhere, including shops, exhibitions, and fair locations.

www.ruffandcut.com
Ethical rough-cut Canadian diamond rings made using recycled metals.

www.simplywoodrings.com
Eco-conscious wooden wedding and engagement rings.

www.touchwoodrings.com
Gorgeous, sustainable wooden wedding rings.

www.vintagebeadslaramiestudios.com
Wonderful selection of vintage, costume-jewelry beads.

www.wood-rings.com
Unusual and ethical composite wooden rings.

Jewelry and other craft workshops

These can be great places to learn skills or host alternative bachelorette parties.

www.craftzine.com
Projects, forums, and news about classes and events nationwide.

www.makeworkshop.com
From earrings to crochet, soap to screen printing, based in Manhattan.

www.etsy.com
Enjoy Etsy Labs craft nights in Brooklyn and San Francisco, or find beautiful things from other makers.

www.homeecshop.com
Craft shop and classes in Silverlake, Los Angeles.

www.themakesite.com
Boutique and contemporary craft classes in Dallas, Texas.

www.theurbancraftcenter.com
Sociable crafting and parties in Santa Monica, California.

Invites

www.bellafigura.com
Classic and contemporary letterpress invites printed on cotton paper made from reclaimed fibers.

www.dauphinepress.com
Elegant designs printed by ecofriendly letterpress.

www.earthlyaffair.com
Pretty, modern invites responsibly printed on recycled paper.

www.earthinvitations.com
Handmade paper invitations, paper, and DIY kits.

www.botanicalpaperworks.com
Handmade "plantable" paper invites and stationery.

www.charlotterice.com
Fabulous contemporary recycled and ecofriendly invites.

www.green-wedding.net
Tree-free and recycled invites online.

www.invitesite.com
DIY wedding stationery on recycled, tree-free, and handmade papers.

www.oblationpapers.com
Simple and stylish letterpress invites and other stationery.

www.pagestationery.com
Letterpress invites with stylish typography.

www.spilledinkpress.com
Ecochic stationery made using FSC and recycled paper.

Paper and printing

www.conservatree.org
Information on environmentally friendly papers, including photo paper.

www.ecofont.com
New software allowing you to print text using 25 percent less ink.

www.environmentalpaper.org
Information on sustainable paper.

www.greenpaperstudio.com
Environmentally friendly papers.

www.sgppartnership.org
Web site of the Sustainable Green Printing Partnership, including details of member printers.

www.waterless.org
Web site of the Waterless Printing Association, with printers around the country.

E-weddings

www.paperlesspost.com
The coolest e-vites available.

www.greenvelope.com
Classic e-vite designs.

www.weddingwebsites.com
A guide to choosing your wedding Web site, with a listing of providers.

Catering and local food

Find your local artisan producers through the listings sites here or your local publications. Many caterers will offer local, seasonal menus if you ask.

www.ams.usda.gov
Home of the USA's National Organic Program.

www.atlanticbrewing.com
Microbrewery crafting special and seasonal ales and beers.

www.breadalone.com
Artisan-baked bread in New York.

www.eco-bar.net
Mouthwatering organic, mobile cocktail bar.

www.edf.org
Check out their seafood selector for the most sustainable fish.

www.honesttea.com
Organic, fair-trade tea bags and bottled beverages.

www.localharvest.org
Find farmers' markets, farms, and sustainable food in your area.

www.maineventcaterers.com
Carbon-neutral event-catering business based in Arlington, Virginia.

www.montereybayaquarium.org
Useful Web site to help you choose sustainable fish in your region.

www.occasionscaterers.com
Washington, DC–based sustainable caterer using organic, local, and seasonal produce.

www.pickyourown.org
Find pick-your-own fruit farms near you.

www.threetwinsicecream.com
Organic ice cream available in bulk for weddings and events.

www.transfairusa.org
International fair-trade certification.

Cakes

www.cmnycakes.com
New York–based cake baker.

www.edithmeyer.com
Organic cakes from Santa Cruz, California.

www.hellocupcakeonline.com
Cupcakes made using local, seasonal

ingredients, delivered throughout Washington, DC.

www.lusciousorganicdesserts.com
All-natural, organic cakes and desserts, based in California.

www.mallowdrama.com
Organic wedding cakes and truffles, and special diets catering in Reston, Virginia.

www.stickyfingersbakery.com
Delicious vegan cakes and treats.

www.tallanthouse.com
Seattle-based cake baker using organic and seasonal ingredients.

www.whole-cakes.com
Mouthwatering cakes—100 percent organic—in the Bay Area.

Favors

www.botanicalpaperworks.com
"Plantable" seed favors and favor boxes.

www.divinechocolateusa.com
Fair-trade chocolate favors.

www.green-wedding.net
Gorgeous favors, all earth friendly and fair trade.

Flowers

www.ams.usda.gov
The USA's National Organic Program.

www.bohemianbouquets.com
Locally grown flowers and gorgeous bouquets.

www.goodolddaysflorist.com
Organic, locally grown flowers.

www.gorgeousandgreenevents.com
Local and organic bridal flowers.

www.harmonyhillgardens.com
Organic home-grown flowers.

www.locoflo.com
Local, sustainable florist based
in Baltimore.

www.lovenfreshflowers.com
Gorgeous home-grown cut-flower
florist in Philadelphia.

www.organicstyle.com
Certified organic and VeriFlora flowers.

www.robinhollowfarm.com
Locally grown cut flowers.

www.soulflowersf.com
Supporting local and organic
flower farms, based in San Francisco.

www.tiarefloraldesign.com
Fair-trade, organic, and sustainable
floral design, Tacoma, Washington.

www.transfairusa.org
International fair-trade
certification organization.

www.veriflora.com
Sustainable flowers and horticulture.

www.wisterialaneflowershop.com
Elegant organic arrangements.

Decorations

www.allsopgarden.com
Pretty hanging solar lanterns.

www.beeswaxcandles.com
Beeswax and soy-wax
natural candles.

www.branchingoutt.com
Recovered tree-branch decorations.

www.ecolecticevents.com
Ecofriendly decorations.

www.eluckyme.com
Wedding Web site with ideas and
templates for DIY decorations
and favors.

www.etsy.com/shop/KristinaMarie
Recycled garlands made from maps
and old paper.

www.green-wedding.net
Site of green wedding products
available to buy online.

www.nimli.com
Ecohomewares, candles, and
decorations.

www.skylanterns.com
Biodegradable flying lanterns.

www.westelm.com
This online store has a green section
with storm lanterns.

Natural beauty

www.barefoot-botanicals.com
Try their rose-scented body-sculpt
body cream for defined curves.

www.comvitahuni.com
Delicious Huni skin care, which uses
manuka honey.

www.decadentbeauty.com
Natural and organic beauty brands.

www.drhauschka.com
Established natural skin-care brand.

www.futurenatural.com
Online shop selling organic and
natural beauty products.

www.jowoodorganics.com
Gorgeous perfumes for organic girls.

www.jurlique.com
Australian beauty products and the
best body scrub available.

www.lavera.com
Fabulous, affordable natural makeup
and skin care; Touch of Sun is a
beauty- bag must.

www.lavere.co.uk
Ethical skin care designed for
thirtysomethings-plus.

www.livingnature.com
Pure skin care from New Zealand.

www.logona.co.uk
Makeup and skin care—they produce
the iconic wrinkle-therapy cream.

www.luzernlabs.com
Luxury natural skin care that
delivers results.

www.naturisimo.com
Online natural beauty store.

www.nealsyardremedies.com
Organic skin care with online store.

www.nudeskincare.com
The best natural makeup remover
available; try their night oil, too.

www.purist.com
Bath and body products for bride and
groom from A'kin.

www.skinbotanica.com
Gorgeous natural beauty.

www.theorganicpharmacy.com
Home of organic skin care and
makeup.

www.weleda.com
Established superethical
skin-care brand.

Registries

www.changingthepresent.org
Select from charities benefiting
causes from animal protection to
human rights.

www.giveincelebration.org
Cancer Research Web site for gift
donations and favors.

www.idofoundation.org
Charity-linked registries.

www.justgive.org
Charitable wedding registries.

www.justgiving.com
Charity donation Web site.

www.oxfamamericaunwrapped.com
Many alternative gifts that benefit less
developed countries.

www.rainforestconcern.org
Sponsor an acre of rainforest.

www.rowemountain.com
Fabulous fair-trade gifts
and homewares.

Honeymoon

Also see the hotel resources listed
under Venues.

www.ecofriendlyhotels.co.uk
Ecofriendly hotels all over the world.

www.ecotourism.org
Home of the International
Ecotourism Society.

www.elevatedestinations.com
Responsible travel destinations.

www.energystar.gov
Find energy-efficient hotels.

www.greentraveller.co.uk
This Web site is all you need to plan
your green break.

www.organicholidays.co.uk
Fabulous organic hotels, farm, and
self-catering accommodation
across the world.

www.responsibletravel.co.uk
The world's leading travel agent for
responsible holidays.

www.seat61.com
How to travel the world by train
and ship.

www.uplandescapes.com
Ecofriendly walking holidays.

Carbon offsetting

www.carbonfund.org
Offset your carbon footprint here.

www.climatecare.org
Credible carbon-offset company.

Green Web sites

www.ecofashionworld.com
Information and directory of
ecobrands and ecostores.

www.eere.energy.gov
US Department of Energy's information
Web site on green energy.

www.epa.gov/greenvehicles
Look up your wedding vehicle online
to check its emissions.

www.gengreenlife.com
Search the green business directory.

www.greenyour.com
How to make many areas of your life
more ecofriendly—including travel
and weddings.

www.sierraclubgreenhome.com
General green-information Web site.

www.treehugger.com
From environment and ecodesign
news to buyers' guides.

Glossary

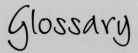

BDIH
The European organization that certifies beauty products as being natural (www.kontrollierte-naturkosmetik.de).

Biomass boiler
A boiler powered by wood chips or pellets that can be used to heat water or as part of a central-heating system.

Carbomers
Synthetic polymers, or plasticlike substances, used to thicken cosmetics and stop them from separating.

DEAs
Compounds of diethanolamine, which have a range of uses in cosmetics and skin-care products. Also look for TEA, or triethanolamine. There are concerns that these can react with certain other ingredients to form cancer-causing chemicals, which have led to restrictions on how they can be used.

DBP
A type of phthalate.

Ecocert
French organic and sustainability certification body for food, cosmetics, and textiles (www.ecocert.com).

Embodied energy
The total energy required to make a product, from extraction and manufacture to transport. Some analyses also include the energy required to disassemble and dispose of the product after use.

GMOs
Genetically modified organisms.

Mineral oil
Also listed as paraffinum liquidum. Clear, odorless oil derived from petroleum. Believed to interfere with the body's own protective oily barrier.

OFC
Organic Food Chain, an Australian certification body (www.organicfoodchain.com.au).

Parabens
Widely used as artificial preservatives in cosmetics. There is concern that some may be carcinogenic.

Phthalates
Used as softeners in plastics but found widely in products such as hairspray and perfumes.

SLS
Sodium lauryl sulfate is a harsh and potentially skin-irritating detergent used as a foaming agent in shampoos and toothpaste. Some natural products use sodium laureth sulfate as an alternative, but there are questions about this compound, too.

Sulfates
A catchall term employed to mean detergents such as sodium lauryl and laureth sulfates and other similar compounds. Not all chemicals listed on labels as a sulfate are detergents.

USDA
The US Department of Agriculture, which oversees and sets the regulations for organic certification in the United States (www.usda.gov).

Note:
The use of all chemicals in cosmetics is under constant review and regulation by organizations such as the US Food and Drug Administration (www.fda.gov).

Seasonal Fruit and Vegetables

Note that January includes some produce that comes into season late in the year but continues to be available through winter.

January

Vegetables
Cabbages
Cauliflower
Cavolo nero
Jerusalem artichokes
Kale
Purple sprouting broccoli

Fruit
Champagne rhubarb
Late pears, such as
    Conference
Seville oranges for
    marmalade and other
    citrus fruits

February

Vegetables
Greenhouse lettuces

March

Vegetables
Chives
Nettles
Watercress

April

Vegetables
Early baby salad leaves and
    winter lettuce
Radishes
Sorrel
Spinach
Wild garlic

May

Vegetables
Asparagus
New potatoes
New season carrots
Wild rocket

June

Vegetables
Autumn-planted onions
Broad beans
Lettuces
Peas and mangetout
Tomatoes from greenhouses

Fruit (and flowers)
Cherries
Elder flowers
Gooseberries
Red currants
Strawberries

July

Vegetables
Artichokes
Beetroot
Cauliflower
Chanterelle mushrooms
French and runner beans
Garlic
Onions
Tomatoes grown outdoors
Zucchini

Fruit
Black currants
Blueberries
Raspberries

August

Vegetables
Broccoli
Chard
Cucumbers
Eggplants
Fennel
Oyster mushrooms
Porcini mushrooms
Sweet corn

Fruit
Apples (early varieties)
Apricots
Autumn raspberries
Blackberries
Damsons
Plums

September

Vegetables
Borlotti beans and other
    pulses for drying
Cabbages
Chilies
Kale
Peppers
Squashes and pumpkins

Fruit
Apples
Elderberries
Greengages
Pears

Nuts
Hazelnuts

October

Vegetables
Celeriac

Fruit
Apples for storing over
    the winter
Crab apples
Grapes
Quinces
Sloes

Nuts
Walnuts

November

Vegetables
Brussels sprout tops
Cavolo nero
Chicory and radicchio
Jerusalem artichokes
Parsnips
Swedes

Nuts
Chestnuts

December

Vegetables
Brussels sprouts
Spring greens

Fruit
Champagne rhubarb
    (forced)
Citrus fruits

Seasonal Flowers

January

Dogwood stems
Hellebores
Hyacinths grown indoors
Snowdrops
Winter cherry blossom
Witch hazel stems in flower

February

Camellias
Dwarf irises
Narcissi (early)
Ornamental quince blossom

March

Catkins and
   willow branches
Cherry blossom
Daffodils
Forsythia
Hyacinths
Tulips
Wood anemones

April

Forget-me-nots
Fritillaries
Lily of the valley
Magnolia
Plum and apple blossom
Violets in pots and for
   edible blossoms

May

Alliums
Bluebells
Bupleurums
Calendula
Calla lilies
Campanulas
Cornflowers
Cow parsley and
   other umbellifers
Foxgloves
Irises
Lady's mantle
Lilac
Oriental poppies
Peonies
Roses
Snapdragons
Stocks
Sweet peas

June

Astrantias
Lavender
Monardas
Nigella
Sweet williams

July

Bells of Ireland
Cosmos
Delphiniums
Hydrangeas
Lilies
Phlox
Scabious
Zinnias

August

Echinaceas
Fresh hops
Grasses
Love-lies-bleeding
Sunflowers

September

Agapanthus
Asters
Dahlias
Eryngiums
Japanese anemones
Sedums

October

Hips and crab apples
Maples and other
   autumn foliage
Nerines

November

Chrysanthemums
Pansies
Winter-flowering
   honeysuckle stems

December

Amaryllis grown indoors
Cyclamen in pots
Holly
Ivy
Paperwhite narcissi
   grown indoors
Viburnum blossom stems

If you do buy imported flowers, look for the following accreditations to make sure they are grown in a socially and environmentally responsible way:

EcoBlooms
VeriFlora
FAIRTRADE
Transitional
Florverde
Ecocert
Rainforest Alliance
Fair Labor Practices
FlorEcuador

Index

Acknowledgments

I would like to express my thanks to everyone who has been involved in this book, right from the start; my sincere appreciation goes out to them all.

Firstly, to my gorgeous friends who agreed to model for us: Lauren Bunclark, Emma Savage, Karen Matthews, Esther Lincoln, Sophie Shenstone, Vicky Millar, Maya Gavin, Jo Illsley, and Rachel Wardley, along with newlyweds Lisa and Pedro, and Tom and Clare; flower girls Sadie and Angelica; and the garden-party wedding guests. You were all stars, even in the rain.

Secondly, to our professional team of wedding specialists who all so kindly gave their time: Karen and Lee Matthews from Lee Matthews Hair Studio Ltd., Rachel Hill from Planet Cake, Joanna Sinska from Josi, and Rachel Wardley from Tallulah Rose Flowers.

Thirdly, a huge thank-you to my best friend, Justyn Turnbull, who let us invade his house, lent us numerous props from his collection, and cooked us the most delicious food, which can be seen in the Menu chapter.

A big, big thank-you also goes to Caroline Harris, my editor and friend, who has held my hand and guided me through this whole process with patience, sound advice, and many cups of peppermint tea. I would also like to thank Marc Wilson for taking such beautiful photographs, Shelley Doyle for her inspired designs, and editorial assistant Harriet Steeds, who helped enormously.

Finally, I would like to thank my fiancé, Zac. This book really would not have been possible without his constant support, love, serenity, and belief in me and my idea.

Many people and companies have also donated their time or products, or allowed us to use their spaces for the photo shoots. Special thanks go to Jessica Charleston, Jo Illsley at Bath Organic Blooms, Sue Harper at Sweet Loving Flowers, Kate Smith at The Makery, Marylyn and Philip at Rocks East Woodland, Kate Robinson, Janet Meadowcroft and Jill Martin for use of their lovely homes, Adam and Claire Scott-Bardwell, Jessica and Ben Eyers, Louise McGraw, Di Francis of Avonleigh Organic Vineyard, Debbie Coutts from Tattered and Torn, Danaë Duthy of Country Roses, Oxfam Bridal, Nikki from Country Cupcakes, Wendy Morray-Jones, Shropshire Petals, Bramley and Gage, Neal's Yard Remedies, Great Elm Physick Garden, Lavera, Logona, Sante, Elysambre, Peachy Keen Organics, Trevarno, Jonathan Ward, Jo Wood Organics, Mandara, Living Nature, Luzern, A'kin, Nude, Jurlique, Organic Blue, Organic Pharmacy, REN, Butter London, Kimia, and Barefoot Botanicals.

Additional photography: page 25 (sea-glass beads, heart pebbles, beach track) and page 98, Caroline Harris; page 34, © iofoto/Fotolia.com; pages 39 and 202, PapaKåta; pages 41 and 46, Sheepdrove Organic Farm; page 43, Cruck Marquees; page 47, © Marcus Kleppe/Fotolia.com; page 75, family photographs, with thanks to Jackie Carr, Joan and Austen, and Joy and Barry; page 193, © MN Studio/Fotolia.com; page 194, Ruth Brown; page 200, © Marc Wilson/Getty Images.

First published in the United States of America in 2010 by
UNIVERSE PUBLISHING
A Division of Rizzoli International Publications, Inc.
300 Park Avenue South
New York, NY 10010
www.rizzoliusa.com

This book was created by
Harris + Wilson ltd
18 Larkhall Place
Bath BA1 6SF
England
www.harrisandwilson.co.uk

Designed by 20 Twenty Design, www.20twentydesign.co.uk
Edited by Caroline Harris

2010 2011 2012 2013 / 10 9 8 7 6 5 4 3 2 1

ISBN: 978-0-7893-2087-2

Library of Congress Control Number: 2010923744

Printed in China